*SCRIPTWRITING*

*SCRIPTWRITING*

UEA MA

Creative Writing Anthologies

2024

# CONTENTS

| | | |
|---|---|---|
| ALICE NUTTER | *Foreword* | VII |
| JAMES MCDERMOTT | *Introduction* | IX |
| LOUIS CATLIFF | *The Cull* | 2 |
| JOHN DAKIN | *The Prize* | 10 |
| JOSE SOCRATES DELOS REYES | *Wreckage* | 22 |
| ALLAN FARFAN CANALES | *Bodega Bay* | 32 |
| SAMUEL FORDHAM | *The Green* | 42 |
| SARAH GAMBLE | *Sorry for your Trouble* | 46 |
| WENDI GRANTHAM | *The Opposite of a House* | 60 |
| MAZEN HAGGAG | *How Many More Jobs?* | 72 |
| AVA HAMILTON | *Love Life Advice Line* | 86 |
| PHOEBE HAYWOOD | *Lost for Words* | 94 |
| ROSIE JOHNS | *An American is a Creature of Four Wheels* | 106 |
| YAVUZ ORHUN KILIC | *The Sounds of Anxiety* | 116 |
| CHRISTOPHER LINFORTH | *Wildsmith* | 124 |
| MARTHA LOADER | *Splinter* | 134 |
| GRACE MAXTED | *Mummy's Will* | 152 |
| MAE MILBURN | *I'll Be a Boggart to You* | 162 |
| JONATHON SIMS | *Signal Failure* | 168 |
| NINA SUMERLING | *A Convenient Adult* | 176 |
| RIYA VIVEK THORAT | *The Long Shot* | 186 |
| | *Acknowledgements* | 194 |

## ALICE NUTTER
### *Foreword*

Having started a scriptwriting MA in my mid 40's, at a university I won't name because it's 20 years ago and may have improved, I had very mixed feelings about creative writing courses. When I started the MA course I had a deep conviction that it was time to stop everything else and focus on becoming a writer. I was hungry to be pushed and learn craft, but I found I learnt more about thinking like a writer from handouts like Tony Garner's pitch for his show *The Cops* than I did from the taught sessions. And spending 3 hours watching David Farr's, *The Odyssey* on stage showed me more about using fun and absurdity to make a serious point, than any of the lectures.

And there were lectures, writers came in and frequently told us how difficult it was to get a foothold in the creative industries. One person spent an hour telling us how bloody awful it was working on *Eastenders* with scripts going to 17 drafts, and then finished their talk by saying there was no room for new writers in the industry anyway.

A year into my two-year part-time MA course I started to get my first theatre and TV commissions. Working, I was being challenged and picking up craft, things that weren't happening on the course, so I left without finishing. Aware of all the things I didn't know, I set myself to studying scripts and serving an apprenticeship writing on other people's TV shows, along the way learning from mentors like Jimmy McGovern and Simon Beaufoy. I then started co-writing with Simon Beaufoy and executive producing series. Having learnt on the job, I saw the MA course as wasted money.

Seeing the scripts produced on the UEA degree and MA courses, the rigour and enthusiasm of tutors, plus the sheer amount of work the students are willing to do, made me reassess writing courses. Full disclosure, as well as visiting UEA to speak on the MA course and seeing students' rehearsed readings, I've seen the UEA degree and MA up close because my daughter has done both.

Watching the rehearsed readings of UEA's Snoo Wilson degree and MA scriptwriting prize, I saw excellence but the diversity of styles and subject matter spoke of students encouraged to experiment, push boundaries and find their own voice. From cops warring gangsters, to a town torn apart by civil war, African magic realism, to an exploration of the allure of fascism, here were writers producing work that was unique to them. Voice. And voice takes confidence born from a certain amount of talent but also from daring, an understanding of craft and structure (even if all you want to do is understand it enough to turn it on its head) and sheer graft. UEA offers the tools and grasp of what it takes to be a writer: looking at other writers' work to see what's possible. The difficulties, the rewriting, rewriting and rewriting again. The joy when after banging your head against the keyboard for god knows how long, the zone allows you in and you produce something that could only have come from you.

Students start writing courses wanting to be a writer, many will leave UEA knowing that's what they've become. And the supportive group ethos of UEA tutors and students, will be something they carry forward into their working, writing lives. It's not easy earning a living from the thing you love but if a writer has a unique voice, things to say, and a generous attitude towards working with others, with hard work and persistence, that person has more than a slim chance of making their mark. Here's to the writers in this scriptwriting anthology making their mark.

## JAMES MCDERMOTT
### *Introduction*

The work this anthology presents was written by the 2024 Scriptwriting MA cohort. Our first thanks are to the School of Literature, Drama and Creative Writing at UEA and Egg Box Publishing who brought this anthology into existence. They created a platform giving each student a chance to be published and offer the opportunity for curious students to be involved in the publication process. This has been a privilege.

This year's publication would not have been brought to print without the support and perseverance of Nathan Ashman who guided this process from the start. Working with eighteen writers and eight editors, he has been our linchpin and for that we are so grateful.

Next, we would like to express thanks to tutors and supervisors Steve Waters, Ben Musgrave, Sian Evans and James McDermott, each of whom has tailored this programme to their own unique styles and passed on invaluable knowledge and feedback. A shout out to dissertation supervisors Michael Lengsfield, Christabelle Dilks and Richard Hand too. We thank them for their respect and wisdom as we have collaboratively developed our scripts with these wonderful writers, many of whom have had their own fantastic works out this year. Without them, we would not be the writers in this anthology.

This year was James's first year teaching at postgraduate level and what a year it has been. From fantastic classes and now dissertation supervision, he has proven what a brilliant teacher he is as well as a writer and person. His play *Jab* premiered in London this year and was a brave and important portrait of lockdown, provoking many conversations and memories about that time. We appreciate him taking the time to contribute an introduction.

Then there is Alice Nutter, writer and former member of *Chumbawumba*. Her work is often politically charged and examines injustice. Recently, she co-wrote *The Full Monty* for Disney+ with writing partner Simon Beaufoy and has written for radio and theatre, with many plays produced at The West Yorkshire Playhouse. She gave a talk early this year about this career and demonstrated to us that you can be humble *and* successful. Her advice on the importance of persevering as a writer in the face of rejection was particularly impactful and we are grateful for her words then and in this anthology.

Thanks is due also to our editors Riya Thorat, Nina Sumerling, Karen Mayze, Ava Hamilton, Rosie Johns, Yavuz Orhun Kilic, John Dakin and Allan Farfan Canales.

Lastly, a massive thank you to this cohort, full and part-time, who have offered wonderful work, all-important feedback and friendship. It is a tribute to your hard-work and talent that we have such an impressive and diverse anthology to present. It can be intimidating on courses like these where we must lay before a group the work closest to us, but each of you has made this a pleasure. Now we have reached the conclusion of our course, our names and work are in these pages as testament to our time together.

Here's wishing the very best for everyone's post-postgraduate future!

# SCRIPTWRITING

THE CULL

(An animated short film)

Written by

Louis Catliff

Louis Catliff is a multi-award-winning writer and documentary filmmaker with credits in stage, screen and radio. He's had a TV pilot shortlisted for the BBC Drama room, a radio monologue produced by the Painkiller Podcast and is developing a one-woman show with Menagerie Theatre. He writes darkly comic, politically engaged work.

lcatliff@gmail.com

FADE IN:

EXT. COAST, SCOTLAND — MORNING

A picturesque strip of beach. Windswept and wild.

Over the dunes stands an enormous sign proclaiming: DUNHOLME 5-STAR HOTEL AND SPA coming soon.


INT. WOODLAND, COAST, SCOTLAND - CONTINUOUS

Between the treeline and the dunes, stands a man in heavy boots and a hard hat, JAMIE (40s), talking to two other men holding chainsaws. He gestures to an area of trees. They rev up and start cutting, wood chips flying everywhere.

A small group of protestors are gathered behind a nearby fence, waving signs saying — DUNES BEFORE POUNDS, PROTECT OUR COASTS, EAT THE RICH Etc.

Nestled in a nearby dune are a pair of seagulls; one little, one large with matching bursts of brown forehead feathers.

Jamie is inspecting a map with plans drawn out for the area - the dunes and woodland marked in red for demolition.

A notification dings. He folds up the map and digs out his phone.

On it we read:

'You've got a Match!' - above a photo of a pretty blonde woman. A smile curls on Jamie's lips. He begins to type.

We return to the seagulls. Their beady eyes narrowing.


EXT. SANDWICH SHOP, MAIN STREET, SEASIDE TOWN - DAY

Jamie struts out of a posh sandwich shop, holding a heaving baguette. He goes to take a bite when a seagull swoops down and plucks it from his hands.

He reels away before gathering himself. He catches the eye of two grizzled nearby day drinkers. He tries to laugh it off but they remain stony-faced. From the rooftops, the brown feathered seagull watches, the baguette clutched in its beak.

EXT. TWEED SHOP, MAIN STREET, SEASIDE TOWN - MIDDAY

Jamie steps out of the tweed shop. Nervous. He checks the skies. All clear. Phew.

He straightens his arms, admiring his brand-new jacket. Perfect fit. A white-brown shit splatters his shoulder. The stony-faced drinkers chuckle.

                    JAMIE

    Grrrr...


EXT. BARBERSHOP, EAST STREET, SEASIDE TOWN - AFTERNOON

Jamie leaves a posh looking barbershop. His hair is freshly trimmed and coiffed and he's thought ahead, producing an umbrella from his pocket. He goes to put it up when it jams. He tries forcing it open, but a seagull swoops and snatches it from his hands.

                    JAMIE

    Ah!

Another gull shits on his head.

                  JAMIE (CONT'D)

    AAAARGH!

He wheels round, scanning the tops of the buildings. He spots the brown headed gull with a flock of others. They open their beaks and caw at him, their mocking cries mingling with the laughs of the drinkers and echoing in his ears.


INT. SEAFOOD RESTAURANT, WEST STREET, SEASIDE TOWN - NIGHT

Jamie is sat at a table. Candles flickering. Glass full of wine. His hair is a little damp, a faint stain on the shoulder of his tweed jacket.

He's sat across from the WOMAN he matched with earlier. Her lips move but Jamie's not listening. His gaze drifts past her shoulder to focus on the window of the restaurant that faces the street. One hundred pairs of beady bird eyes stare back at him out of the darkness. Glittering with menace.

His knee bounces up and down as he brings the menu up to shield himself from their gaze. Everything on it reads:

*CAW, CAW, CAW, CAW.*

The shadow of the WAITER passes over Jamie. His DATE asks something - muffled as if she's underwater. Jamie looks up.

                    JAMIE
    Hm?

He lowers the menu to reveal a GIANT SEAGULL staring at him, its head and neck protruding from his DATE's human body.

                  SEAGULL DATE
    CAW!

                    JAMIE
    AH!

Jamie reels back, sending his wine crashing to the floor. The entire restaurant falls silent and turns to stare. His DATE looks away. Embarrassed. Jamie lowers his eyes.


EXT. SEAFOOD RESTAURANT, WEST STREET - CONTINUOUS

The DATE checks her phone. We read on it: *'No Driver Available.'*

Jamie is cowering beneath the awning over the restaurant's entrance. The DATE sighs, putting away her phone and turning to go. Jamie grabs her hand, shaking his head in terror. She gives him a look of disgust before tugging her hand free and striding off.

Jamie watches her walk down the street and disappear. He takes a deep breath and steps out into the road. Nothing. He takes another step and another. He breaks into a trot, his confidence growing. He laughs. Everything's fine! He's safe! Suddenly, a storm of seagulls descends, whirling around him. They peck and claw and tear at his clothes. He screams and sprints off down the street.


EXT. JAMIE'S FLAT, MAIN STREET - MOMENTS LATER

Jamie skids to a halt outside a door, jams in a key, yanks it open and flings himself inside.

INT. ENTRANCE HALL, JAMIE'S FLAT, MAIN STREET - CONTINUOUS

A ragged, poo covered Jamie turns to peer out the peephole. The silhouettes of hundreds of seagulls crowd every rooftop. One swoops down, scratching at the peephole.

SEAGULL
CAW!

Jamie tumbles backwards. Something cracks as he lands. He takes out his phone to reveal a shattered screen. Sighs.

INT. LIVING ROOM, JAMIE'S FLAT - NIGHT

Jamie is sat, hollow-eyed and shaking beneath a blanket. In front of him is a half-eaten plate of chips and egg lit by the flickering TV on which an old Sci-Fi film is playing.

In it, a man sprints down a corridor, lasers flying overhead. A robot trundles after him yelling:

ROBOT
EXTERMINATE! EXTERMINATE!

Jamie leans forward, raising a chip to eye-level. An idea is forming.

INT. KITCHEN, JAMIE'S FLAT — CONTINUOUS

Jamie rushes into the kitchen and cranks up the oven to MAX!

He grabs bags of chips from the freezer, rips them open and dumps the contents onto a pair of baking trays which he thrusts into the oven.

He gathers salt and pepper before yanking open a cupboard below the sink to reveal a heaving sack labelled RAT POISON.

A timer dings. Jamie draws the smoking, golden-brown chips from the oven. Teeth gritted and eyes glinting, he sprinkles on the seasonings before showering them in poison.

INT. LIVING ROOM, JAMIE'S FLAT - CONTINUOUS

Jamie goes to his living room window, overlooking the main

street. He flings it wide and scatters chips over the street below.

Seconds tick by. All is still. Then the shadow of a seagull flits across the window swooping down to pick up a chip. Another gull swoops and another. Suddenly the streets are a storm of gulls all pecking and gulping.

JAMIE smiles, the flap of wings reflected in his eyes.

EXT. MAIN STREET, SEASIDE TOWN - MORNING

The sun rises. A terrible chorus of caws splits the air - full of misery and pain.

Jamie struts through the mass of dying seabirds, twitching on their backs. He comes to one. Brown forehead feathers. His nemesis. The seagull looks up at him, beak frothing. Jamie raises a heavy boot and brings it down hard. Crunch!

EXT. ROOFTOP, SEASIDE TOWN - CONTINUOUS

A TINY SEAGULL with the same brown forehead feathers watches in horror. As the cries of the gulls mingle together, he flaps frantically, taking to the skies.

The tiny Seagull flies over the rooftops and beaches, the woodland and ice-cold ocean all the way to a vast craggy rock, rising out of the sea.

EXT. SEAGULL ISLAND, NORTH SEA — CONTINUOUS

The TINY SEAGULL struggles against the gale force wind, dipping low before powering himself back up and disappearing into the deep, dark hole in the cliffside.

INT. SEAGULL ISLAND, NORTH SEA - CONTINUOUS

The seagull glides down the tunnel before, at last, his wings give out and he tumbles to the floor rolling to a stop at the bottom of a giant nest. Inside, we see the steady rise and fall of a fully grown SEAGULL's feathery chest. We can't tell its exact size, but it's big. Very big.

The cries of the TINY SEAGULL wake THE BIG ONE. It blinks its vast black eyes, sleep turning to rage as the tiny seagull delivers one final, desperate 'CAW' before passing out.

EXT. SEAGULL ISLAND, NORTH SEA — CONTINUOUS

A feathered shadow rushes past our view, blotting out the sun for a second.

EXT. MAIN STREET, SEASIDE TOWN - MIDDAY

JAMIE trots out of the fish and chip shop. A red cashmere scarf draped around his neck. He tosses one end of it carelessly over his shoulder before raising his box of chips and delicately skewering one with a tiny wooden fork. He pops it in his mouth and chews. Triumphant.

A shadow passes across Jamie. He shivers. The sound of wingbeats fills the air. He looks up to see the outline of a seagull bearing down on him, silhouetted against the sun.

Jamie smiles and shakes his head. He grabs a shaker labelled 'EMERGENCY POISON' from his pocket. He tips it vigorously over the chips before raising the Styrofoam box aloft.

A few seconds pass, the shadow over Jamie grows larger and larger until he is entirely bathed in shade. Something's wrong. Too late. He opens his mouth to scream when —

EXT. MAIN STREET, SEASIDE TOWN - MOMENTS LATER

The chip box lies face down on the ground, food scattered. We hear screams, faint and growing fainter. Jamie's red cashmere scarf floats down into view, settling on the ground.

In the distance we can make out a bird flying over rooftops and out to sea, something live and wriggling in its claws.

**THE END**

THE PRIZE

(A Short Film)

Written by

John Dakin

John Dakin is a writer and freelance journalist based in the UK. Getting his start as a theatre director and script editor, John always found himself chasing after stories that appealed to him, whether in fiction or based off the surreal experiences found in everyday life and our popular culture. Formerly working as the editor and producer of the highly successful New European Podcast, John Dakin is currently attending the MA Scriptwriting course at UEA, after previously having graduated with a First in Film and Television studies also from UEA. While studying he has written several short films, one of which is currently being produced in conjunction with The Sainsbury's Centre for Visual Arts.

Johndakin00@gmail.com

EXT. DREAMZONE ARCADE, DAY.

*A crummy neon sign flickers aimlessly in the midday sun, letters spelling out "Dreamzone", the D styled to look like the planet Saturn. Though seemingly barren inside, the lights remain on.*

*Across the lot a lone car pulls up, tires trampling over a discarded soda cup.*

*MACKENZIE looks at herself in the rear-view mirror for a moment. Mid-Late 20's, dishevelled, a weariness about her. On her jacket, there's a large button that reads "birthday girl".*

*Looking up at the sign, she smiles and takes a breath before glancing over to her glove compartment.*

CUT TO:


INT. DREAMZONE ARCADE, MOMENTS LATER.

*The tinny sound of retro game music fills the air as several faded arcade machines whir incessantly. Blinking lights and flashing screens.*

*MANNY lays his head on the desk of the token exchange desk on the far side, bored out of his mind. Suddenly, a broom crashed down on his head.*

                    MANNY
    Huh? Carlos, what the fuck?

*Manny raises his head. Late teens, acne ridden, ratty blonde hair. A taller Latino man wearing the same awful employee vest as him looms overhead, holding a broom like a spear.*

                    CARLOS
    If you can't find something to do,
    look harder! You think I get to go
    shut my eyes and sit in the corner
    going "mimimimimimimimi" while
    snoring like a pig? No man, I'm the
    assistant fucking manager now.

*He points to a pin on his vest. Manny doesn't seem amused.*

MANNY
How can you be an assistant manager if there are only four employees?

CARLOS
Five actually. Kevin locks the place up.

MANNY
Yeah, cuz he's Rich's son.

CARLOS
Look just, help me out here man. Richard is counting on me now. At least look like you're doing something?

MANNY
Fine, whatever. It's not like anybody comes in on a-

*The pair pause as Mackenzie walks through the automatic door. Time seems to slow as she brushes a hand through her hair like a model. The boys are instantly enamoured.*

MANNY
A girl…

CARLOS
A girl…

*The pair look at each other for a moment, eyes narrowed.*

MANNY
Dream on hombre.

CARLOS
Don't try me bro. I could get your ass fired.

MANNY
For what, hitting on the same girl as you?

*Carlos holds his broom threateningly.*

CARLOS
Don't you get it bro? This girl plays retro games!

MANNY
So what?

CARLOS
So what? Man, someone better check
out your head. Girl like that comes
around once in a lifetime.

*Manny smirks.*

MANNY
How about we make it a little
contest? Player One vs Player Two.

CARLOS
You mean...

MANNY
Shoot your shot homie. Let's see who
she likes more. An ageing fatass or-

*Carlos slams his broom down on Manny's counter, making him jump.*

CARLOS
Or a pimply little punk who's still
on minimum wage and can't even buy
her a beer. Alright, deal.

MANNY
Go on then, show her the "assistant
manager charm".

*Carlos gives Manny the finger as he walks over to Mackenzie with a big grin on his face.*

*Mackenzie looks around, taking in the ambiance of the arcade and closing her eyes. Carlos appears in front of her suddenly.*

CARLOS
Hey! Welcome to... THE DREAMZONE!
My name is Carlos, how can I-

MACKENZIE
(screaming)
Aaaah!

*Mackenzie reaches for something in her pocket, a terrified look on her face.*

CARLOS
Woah! Sorry ma'am I just-

MACKENZIE
B-back up. Back up right now.

*Carlos does so as Mackenzie takes a breath, putting her hands on her knees.*

MACKENZIE
Okay. What do you want?

CARLOS
Well. I just wanted to welcome you to the-

MACKENZIE
Okay. I'm welcomed. Thank you.

*Carlos scratches the back of his neck awkwardly.*

CARLOS
Uh, well if you need anything. I'm the-

MACKENZIE
Is that a broom in your hand?

*Carlos looks down, remembering he still has the broom.*

CARLOS
Oh uh, yes it is!

MACKENZIE
I wouldn't want to be keeping you from doing your job then, Carlos.

*Mackenzie passes him like the wind. Dejected, Carlos begins sweeping.*

*Mackenzie runs her hand along an old pinball machine as she weaves through various rows of arcade cabinets, her face lit up by flashing screens.*

*Manny gazes at her dreamily as she walks up to him.*

*Mackenzie gives him a nod for a moment and looks like she's about to speak, when a crane machine in the corner catches her eye. Atop a pile of stuffed animal toys sits an octopus.*

MANNY
Uh, ma'am?

*Mackenzie's eyes are suddenly wide, bug-like. All the colour has drained from her face.*

MANNY
Ma'am!

*In an instant, she cracks her neck towards Manny.*

MACKENZIE
Hmm?

MANNY
Can I help you with something?

*A pause.*

MACKENZIE
Sorry. I guess I was just getting a little nostalgic.

*Manny tries his best to offer a weak laugh, leaning on the counter slightly.*

MANNY
No problem. Did you uh, used to come here a lot?

*Mackenzie trembles.*

MACKENZIE
Yeah. That was a long time ago.

MANNY
Well uh, it's nice to have you back ma'am.

*Mackenzie gives him a small smile.*

MACKENZIE
It's Mackenzie. It's my birthday today.

*She points to the large badge on her jacket. Manny smiles.*

MANNY
Awesome! Happy birthday Mackenzie.

*Mackenzie twiddles a ringlet of her hair nervously.*

> MACKENZIE
> Oh, uh. Thanks.

> MANNY
> Sooooo... Do you have any friends
> coming along?

*Mackenzie's face drops. Instantly, she slams a hand down on the table in front of Manny. He gulps.*

> MACKENZIE
> Are you mocking me?

*Manny raises his hands defensively.*

> MANNY
> No no, I was just asking if-

> MACKENZIE
> (coldly)
> I need the bathroom.

*Manny nods apologetically.*

> MANNY
> Uh, they're just over there on the-

> MACKENZIE
> I fucking know where they are.

*Mackenzie storms off. Manny puts his head down on the desk sadly. Carlos begins to sweep over towards him with a smug look on his face.*

> CARLOS
> You totally blew it man.

> MANNY
> Yeah well, so did you.

*Carlos sweeps away from him while humming a tune, raising a finger.*

> CARLOS
> (singing)
> Not as bad as you hombre!

*Manny just rolls his eyes, looking over at the crane machine.*

*The octopus stares back at him with lifeless eyes.*

INT. LADIES BATHROOM, MOMENTS LATER.

*Mackenzie sits motionless in one of the toilet stalls, calming her breathing.*

*Looking down to one of her hands, she notices it twitching slightly.*

                    MACKENZIE
     Fucking... Asshole. Where are YOUR
     friends?

*A moment later, a toilet is flushed as she emerges from the stall and slowly walks over to the sink.*

*Flicking on the warm water, she begins washing her hands. Pausing for a moment as she notices herself in the mirror.*

*Noticing her badge, Mackenzie looks down at it and smiles. When her eyes return to the mirror, she sees a little girl standing behind her with an identical badge.*

                    LITTLE GIRL
     Did you forget what you're here for?

*Mackenzie simply shakes her head, paralyzed with fear.*

                    LITTLE GIRL
     It's here. Just like I said it would
     be. All you have to do is take it.
     You're a big girl now.

*Mackenzie nods, gripping something in her jacket pocket as she stares at the girl.*

                    LITTLE GIRL
        (shouting)
     Well? What are you waiting for? Go!

*Mackenzie turns around to look at the girl, only to find nobody there. Determined, she storms out of the bathroom.*

INT. DREAMZONE ARCADE, MOMENTS LATER.

*Manny sheepishly adjusts the positions of some prizes behind him. He notices Mackenzie walk out of the bathroom and make a beeline towards him fast.*

*Carlos notices, giving Manny a smug look as he mouths "good luck" to him.*

*Mackenzie stands in front of Manny, her face deathly serious. Manny begins to stammer out an apology.*

              MANNY
Hey. Look, I'm sorry about how that came across. Really, I was just asking because I thought it would be nice to-

*Click. Manny looks down, sees the gun pressed up to his chest. Mackenzie doesn't move, doesn't even flinch. Manny's breath catches in his throat. On instinct, he raises his hands.*

              MACKENZIE
Give it to me. Everything

*Carlos freezes, his hands grip at his broom tightly as he stares at Manny with horror.*

*Manny's eyes flicker to Carlos for a second before looking at the woman and nodding, slowly moving his hand to the cash register.*

*Enraged, Mackenzie fires, knocking off a toy rocket on the shelf behind him.*

              MACKENZIE
I. don't want. Your fucking. Chump change. I'm here to play.

*Manny ducks his head down, holding back tears.*

              MANNY
I'm sorry I, I don't understand.

              MACKENZIE
Tokens. Give me every last token you have back there. I swear to god if you leave one, I will blow your fucking head off.

*Manny looks at her, eyes wide. Unable to process.*

                    MANNY
    You-

                  MACKENZIE
    I want the fucking tokens!

*Manny scrunches up his eyes and begins slamming tokens down on the counter. Mackenzie relaxes a little.*

                  MACKENZIE
    More. I need more of them.

                  MANNY
    Okay! Okay... Just please, calm
    down.

*Manny indicates to Carlos. Carlos slowly begins to approach, holding the broom in both hands.*

*Mackenzie's eyes lazily scan the tokens as she grabs a handful and stuffs them into her pockets.*

*Without a word, she moves backwards towards the crane machine and places a token inside it. Gun still poised at Manny.*

*The machine suddenly whirs back to life. Carlos and Manny exchange a dumbfounded look as Mackenzie turns towards the machine and begins to play. A cackle escapes her lips.*

                  MACKENZIE
      (laughing)
    Twenty years. It's been twenty
    fucking years, and nobody ever got
    you.

*She puts her hand towards the octopus and runs it down the glass longingly.*

                  MACKENZIE
    Well not anymore. I'm back, and I'm
    going to take you home. No matter
    how many times it takes me.

*She begins to move the crane towards the octopus. The mechanical arm clamps down around it, pulling it up slightly before a tentacle slips from grasp.*

MACKENZIE
Fuck! Again.

*She goes for another token. Another failure, another scream.*

MACKENZIE
C'monnnnnnn baby I've got all night!

*Mackenzie continues to play, the gun going slack in her hand as she focuses on the game.*

*Carlos looks over to Manny, indicating with his hand that he should go for his phone. Manny shakes his head, pointing to the employee's room in the back, locked with a push button handle.*

*Carlos silently clenches his fist before looking over to the mad woman. He indicates to Manny with his fingers that he's going to tiptoe over and smack her with the back of the broom.*

*Manny tries to shake his head, but Carlos just gives him a salute. Slowly he begins to move towards Mackenzie, who still has her back turned. His walk breaks into a run.*

*Mackenzie continues hammering away at the crane as Carlos charges at her from behind with the broom raised over his head. In an instant, the smile fades and she whips around, cracking the butt of the pistol against his nose. He drops.*

*Mackenzie looks into Manny's eyes as she raises the gun towards him. Manny stares back. His eyes briefly wander over to an arcade machine. The words "GAME OVER" stare back at him in bright red text. The Octopus watches on passively.*

MACKENZIE
Now. Where were we?

WRECKAGE

(A 10-minute play)

Written by

Jose Socrates Delos Reyes

Jose Socrates Delos Reyes is a Filipino educator and playwright. He graduated with a BFA in Creative Writing from the Ateneo de Manila University and is an alumnus of Tanghalang Ateneo, the university's longest-running theater company. His works tackle politics, trauma, and oppression. His plays have been staged in the Philippines and the UK.

j.socdelosreyes@gmail.com

> *"The fishermen [...] keep coming back to cast their nets. Along its shores, entangled among the corals, are shreds of clothes, blankets and mosquito nets, toys and many other parts of their lives."*
>
> *—Jane Subang*

> *"A YEAR AFTER: New village rising where 120 died"*
>
> *Philippine Daily Inquirer December 2004*

**CHARACTERS**

INDAY – 15-16 years old, stepdaughter

RICARDO – mid-40s, stepfather, fisherman

**SETTING**

In a coastal village in the Philippines. 2003.

**PRODUCTION DETAILS**

*Wreckage* was first performed at The Cut Studio in Halesworth, Suffolk, as part of Pod 7 of INK Festival 2024.

DIRECTOR – Mike Bernardin

INDAY – Theresa Jane Knight

RICARDO – Aamer Raza

*Almost noon, in the sea near the coastline. RICARDO and INDAY are in a bangka1 (fishing boat). Ricardo at the front and Inday at the back. Both are rowing slowly. Behind them, tied to the end of the bangka and partially submerged, is a cast net for fishing.*

*Inside, the bloated corpse of a woman.*

*As they're rowing, Ricardo takes a swig from a bottle of gin. Inday stares at his back.*

*Ricardo sees a passing bangka, waves back at them.*

RICARDO: Bai (My friend)! Where are they keeping the bodies? …

Still? The basketball court's full, di ba (isn't it)? Did the body bags from Liloan arrive, at least? … They're what—, blankets and mosquito nets? Ay sus ginoo (My god), what was the gobyerno's (government's) helicopter for, e? Probably waiting for the media for their election coverage no? … Be careful, ha! There's lots of debris. Lots of trees, a roof or two and—

…

Gani (Yes), it's her… Three days missing pero (but) I—

Tanginang landslide ito (This fucking landslide). Buti na lang (It's good that), we still have gin to drown our sorrows with, ano (isn't it)?

*Ricardo raises his bottle as a goodbye. He drinks again.*

INDAY: It wasn't the landslide.

RICARDO: The storms came, and the mountain buried half the town in trees and mud.

INDAY: No, it was a sirena (mermaid) who took her.

RICARDO: Inday…

INDAY: Nanay (Mother) went to the chapel to pray.

The landslide came and she was carried to the sea.

But a sirena (mermaid) took her.

…

RICARDO: Inday, she died in the landslide

INDAY: Then why doesn't she have any wounds?

RICARDO: A story won't bring her back.

| | |
|---|---|
| INDAY: | Her bible's still in her hands she's *smiling* |
| RICARDO: | It was the landslide. |
| INDAY: | Then why was her body upright in the water? |

*… Ricardo takes another swig of gin.*

*A dead body floats. Face down, face up. But she was upright when we found her, her face—her smile—, peeking out of the surface.*

| | |
|---|---|
| RICARDO: | This isn't one of my stories! |
| | It wasn't a sirena (mermaid) or diwata3 (nymph)— |
| | The storm the mountain THEY TOOK HER FROM US. |

*… Inday stops rowing.*

*Ricardo turns to her.*

| | |
|---|---|
| RICARDO: | What? |

*She glares at him.*

        Fine!

*Ricardo stands and moves to the middle of the bangka.*

*He starts rowing.*

*But with the body in the net being dragged behind, the bangka moves languidly.*

*Silence.*

| | |
|---|---|
| RICARDO: | Child, I'm— |
| INDAY: | I'm not your daughter anymore. |
| RICARDO: | Siyempre (Of course) you're still my daughter. |
| | Even if she's— |
| INDAY: | Hindi na. (Not anymore) |
| | Not anymore. |

> Not since you made her leave.

*… Ricardo drinks.*

> Stop it!
>
> All you do is drink! Araw-araw (Every day) drinking your gin like it's water and

RICARDO: You're young, ineng (you don't understand.)

INDAY: That doesn't have anything to do with

RICARDO: It's about getting by

INDAY: Nanay didn't drink, not like you

RICARDO: But she had her bible.

> Her Diyos (God), her statues, her afternoon mahjong with her amigas from church—…
>
> While I worked, we could eat and have something to sell at the palengke (market).

INDAY: She took care of the house. Of us.

RICARDO: She did.

> But I… Kapoy kaayo (I'm exhausted).

*Ricardo shrugs and drinks again.*

INDAY: But why did you have to drink *that* night?

*Ricardo doesn't answer.*

> She left because you came home drunk again.
>
> It's why she went to the chapel, *again*.
>
> Kasi (because) you were screaming and throwing things at each other, and I stayed in my room, closed my eyes covered my ears with my pillow and prayed please tama na (stop) please

>                       tama na (stop)…
>
>                       And she left even in the middle of a storm, to pray—, to beg Jesus at his feet—
>
>                       For you. Nanay (Mother) kept praying for *you*.
>
>                       But you—you still…

*Ricardo can't answer.*

>                       …
>
>                       I used to love your stories.
>
>                       You'd hear me, crying. Even when I tried not to because you were both so angry and—. But you'd sit by me on my banig (mat) and you'd tell me about the sirena (mermaid) or the siyokoy (fishman) you made friends with at sea. Or how you almost drowned in the middle of a storm but the Bakunawa6 came and it let you cling to its scales as it took you to shore.
>
>                       Your breath reeked; it made my nose itchy. But I laughed and I smiled, and I wanted more because *you* made
>                       me feel that things could be okay,
>                       *we* could be okay.
>
>                       Putangina (Fuck), I should've never listened to you.
>
>                       She left. And she's never coming back.
>
>                       …
>
>                       …

RICARDO: It wasn't because I was drunk.

INDAY: You were.

RICARDO: I was.

> But the fight—. Wasn't about that.
>
> I—, she wanted me to sell

|   |   |
|---|---|
| | the bangka. And my nets. My spearguns. Lahat, everything. |
| INDAY: | But-. Why would she make you— |
| RICARDO: | Because it wasn't going to be enough. |
| INDAY: | It was enough for us. |
| RICARDO: | To get by. |
| | But we—, we wanted better for you. We… |
| | Wanted you to go to college, to be a seaman. |
| | In Sogod. Or Liloan… Anywhere that's not here. |
| INDAY: | I don't even want to— |
| RICARDO: | 'Day, we knew. Since last year. When your cousin Joro visited after his first year on a ship. The others, they just wanted to hear about the sweldo (money), the girls, the antics but you— |
| | You spent the night practicing the knots he showed you! |
| INDAY: | It didn't mean anything— |
| RICRADO: | You're a bright child. Brighter than both of us. |
| | You must have gotten it from your tatay (father). |
| INDAY: | You are my tatay (father). |
| RICARDO: | Your first tatay (father), then. Everything here is… still. |
| | You don't see it yet kasi (because) you're young but it is. |
| | Day in and day out, you see the same people, do the same things, hear the same old stories you've been telling each other for years, and the years… |
| | Just keep passing. |
| | It's not a bad life, but it just… |

> is.
>
> And you, you're— you deserve more than this island.
>
> Our daughter, the seaman.
>
> …
>
> There's going to be another mining operation in a few months, right here. There was but—. They were going to hire locals. Steady pay. We thought I could be a miner so I could save up for your future. But…
>
> I got scared. This…

*Ricardo stops rowing and looks at the sea.*

> My tatay (father) was a fisherman. My lolo (grandfather) was a fisherman. It was all my family ever did or could do.
>
> I can take you to the best spots for fishing anywhere, in any season. I can hook squids under the full moon, I know where and when to get sea urchin so fat the meat's bigger than a man's thumb, I can dive, hold my breath, point my speargun just so to hit an octopus hiding under the corals—,
>
> …
>
> But that's all I know.
>
> It's all who I am. Or ever was.
>
> I—, I couldn't…

*Ricardo goes back to rowing.*

> It wasn't a sirena that killed her.
>
> Or the storm. Or the landslide.
>
> She died, because of me.
>
> …
>
> …

*The bangka approaches the coast.*

*Ricardo puts down his paddle and gets out of the bangka. He stands in knee-deep water. He moves to the back of the bangka.*

INDAY: It was a sirena who took her.

*Ricardo stops.*

She prayed and prayed to God for us. To help us. To save us. To take us away to somewhere our stories became real. Then the landslide came

RICARDO: And almost buried her. But the cross saw and went to her,

INDAY: Hand clasped to the bible, she grabbed the cross,

RICARDO: And it carried her through the mud and water…

all the way into the sea.

INDAY: But still, she continued to pray.

RICARDO: For us.

INDAY: So God sent a sirena to help her. It held her,

RICARDO: Cradled her,

INDAY: Kept her safe.

RICARDO: And the sirena took her, away from the muck the filth and the pain

INDAY: And brought her to the sea.

RICARDO: Home.

INDAY: Where she will always be waiting for us.

*Inday gets off the boat to her father's side.*

*The two pull the handline of the net, bringing the body to them.*

*A ritual.*

*Finally, the net-encased body reaches them.*

*They lift and put it in the bangka.*

*Ricardo moves to the opposite side.*

*Together, father and daughter push the bangka to shore.*

BODEGA BAY

A short film script about two brothers trying
to escape from a gruesome time loop.


Written by

Allan Farfan Canales


Allan Farfan Canales is a first-generation Mexican American from Santa Rosa, California. He studied English with minors in Creative Writing and Film & Media Studies at Dickinson College in Pennsylvania and is currently on the MA Creative Writing Scriptwriting course at the University of East Anglia. His favorite subject to write about is Heartbreak and broken relationships. Allan is also interested in exploring questions of Latinidad, family, mental health, sexuality, and the intersectionality of race, class, and gender within his writing and does not restrict himself to a particular genre or medium. He writes, produces, and self-publishes original music under the name ¡Allán! on SoundCloud.

allan.farfan.canales@gmail.com
soundcloud.com/allan_farfan_canales

FADE IN:

EXT. COASTAL HIGHWAY - NIGHT

A white SUV cruises down an American coastal highway. The road is long and winding, with thick coils that twist and taper here and there, threatening to lead the car off the cliffside and into the ocean.

We hear 'Lonely Nights' by *LEISURE* playing from the car speakers.

CAPTION: Bodega Bay, California.

                LEO (O.S.)
          (revelatory gasp)
  Dude, I got it!

CUT TO:

INT. SUV - NIGHT

The SUV has two passengers: ALLAN (early 20s) in the driver's seat, LEO (early teens) in the front seat. Leo is freaking out, like he just discovered the cure for cancer.

                LEO
  You need to crash the car!

Allan glances at him unimportantly.

                ALLAN
  What?

                LEO
  Drive off the road and into the
  ocean.

                ALLAN
  What are you talking about?

                LEO
  Trust me.

                ALLAN
  Hell no, what the fuck?

LEO
I've died like ten thousand times, bro, I can't go through it again. It's gotten *boring*.

ALLAN
Leo, you just had a bad dream. You've been asleep for a while.

LEO
Bro, I'm not making this up. I know everything that's gonna happen.

ALLAN
Like *Groundhog D--*?

LEO
Yes, like the 1993 comedy starring Bill Murray and Andie MacDowell and a poor little groundhog named Punxsutawney Phil.

ALLAN
How do you know about--?

LEO
BECAUSE YOU'VE MANSPLAINED IT TO ME HUNDREDS OF TIMES!

ALLAN
How do you know what 'mansplai--'?

LEO
Allan, I've been in this car with you for so long, reliving the exact same scenario...

ALLAN
I don't believe it.

LEO
In like three seconds, your phone's going to get a text.

Beat.

Allan's cellphone BUZZES. He reaches for it, but Leo slaps his hand away.

                    LEO
          Don't text and drive, that's how
          we die like seventy percent of the
          time.

                    ALLAN
          So, I get us killed? That's fucked.

                    LEO
          'Can't, busy tonight.'

                    ALLAN
          Cold. What else can you predict?

Leo calculates for a moment.

Leo grabs the steering wheel and turns it slightly to the left as they narrowly avoid hitting a cow that's wandered into the road. Allan YELLS as we hear a panning MOOOOOOO.

                    ALLAN
          WHAT THE HELL WAS THAT?

                    LEO
          Does it matter? Whatever happens,
          we always end up in the water.
          Usually, we're trapped in the car
          and drown, but even when we get free
          there's always something crazy.

                    ALLAN
          Like what?

GRUESOME DEATH IN WATER MONTAGE:

... JAGGED ROCKS covered in blood and bone fragments.

... a SHARK FIN circling around a panicked Allan. Leo is missing.

... Leo SCREAMING as Allan's SPRAWLED on a giant stone, his liver being PECKED OUT by a SEAGULL.

... Leo is DRAGGED deeper down into the ocean because his leg is tied to ALLAN's SINKING CORPSE by SEAWEED.

... an explosion of FLASHING LIGHTS as Leo and Allan are electrocuted by JELLYFISH. Underwater fireworks.

END GRUESOME DEATH IN WATER MONTAGE.

                    LEO
          I'll figure out how to avoid an
          obstacle, but then there's a new one
          that kills us.

                    ALLAN
               (shaken)
          Why don't we just pull over? Get out
          the car and walk?

Leo SIGHS.

GRUESOME DEATH ON LAND MONTAGE:

... Allan and Leo walk down the highway and are wiped out by
a TSUNAMI.

... a LANDSLIDE hurdles giant BOULDERS into the road,
KNOCKING them over the cliffside.

... Allan and Leo reached town, but an EARTHQUAKE opens a
CRACK in the ground and they FALL through.

END GRUESOME DEATH ON LAND MONTANGE.

                    ALLAN
          Okay, okay, I get it.

                    LEO
          It's like the Universe doesn't want
          us to survive.

                    ALLAN
          What makes you think this time will
          be different?

                    LEO
          Look, every time we've been trying
          to *avoid* driving off the road, and
          we always end up in the ocean. Where
          we die. Horribly.

                    ALLAN
          What was the worst--


EXT. COASTAL HIGHWAY - MONTAGE OF IMAGES

We see the white SUV driving in its correct lane at the

speed limit. A SPEEDING yellow Mercedes approaches the SUV. Tailgates it. We hear a BEEP. The Mercedes starts passing the SUV. We see Allan's fist emerge from the window, as if he's about to flip the Mercedes off. The Mercedes' passenger window rolls down and a beautiful YOUNG WOMAN lifts her shirt and flashes the brothers. The Mercedes speeds off. Allan STARES, dumbfounded. The SUV misses the curve in the road and drives off the road. The SUV CRASHES head-first into a neighboring cliff and EXPLODES.

INT. SUV - NIGHT

Allan and Leo stare ahead, tight-lipped.

Allan lets out an awkward chuckle that sounds like a cross between a gasp and a sigh.

      ALLAN
  That one didn't sound *that* bad...

      LEO
  Bro, that one actually traumatised
  me. I'm not old enough to see
  *chichis* like that.

Allan lets out a long GROAN.

      LEO (CONT'D)
  Trust me, Allan, I know what I'm
  doing. I'm not afraid of dying
  anymore, but I'm scared of being
  stuck like this forever.

      ALLAN
  Well, *I'm* scared of dying.

      LEO
  Worst-case, the time loop restarts.

      ALLAN
  What if you're making this up?
  Like, you had a nightmare and now
  you're trying to convince me the
  impossible is real.

LEO
Don't insult my intelligence. I'm a straight-A student.

ALLAN
Okay, fine. Let's say we're stuck in a time loop. But what if this time, we go over the edge, and it doesn't restart? And we *die*?

LEO
Then we'll be dead. Finally. And I'll be at peace. Otherwise, nothing matters to me anymore.

ALLAN
Damn. You know, that's called--

LEO
'Nihilism.' I know. You've told me about it. Thousands of times.

ALLAN
I was going to say 'Depression.'

LEO
I used to be depressed. Now, I'm just... done. And really bored.

ALLAN
Have you actually died thousands of times?

LEO
Yes! And it's always to this song.

On cue, 'Out of Time' by *The Weeknd* starts playing.

Allan, mildly surprised but pleased, starts humming along to the instrumental. Leo grimaces: he's been conditioned to feel nauseated by the lead synth.

ALLAN
Yoooo, this song slaps!

LEO
God. Are you ready?

                    ALLAN
               (singing along)
          *THE LAST FEW MONTHS I'VE BEEN*
          *WORKING ON ME BABY--*

                    LEO
          *Allan, are you ready?*

                    ALLAN
               (singing along)
          *THERE'S SO MUCH TRAUMA IN MY LI--*

                    LEO
          *ALLAN!*

                    ALLAN
               (annoyed)
          Leo, there's no way I'm--

                    LEO
          Aight, Kobe!

Leo GRABS the wheel and SPINS it to point the car towards the highway railing. He lifts himself up and with his free hand, brings his weight down on Allan's right leg, to FLOOR the gas pedal.

The engine ROARS in response and the car ACCELERATES.

                    ALLAN
          LEO, WHAT ARE YOU DOING?

                    LEO
          As soon as we're in the air, undo
          your seatbelt and open the door!

                    ALLAN
          THIS IS INSANE, LET GO--

The SUV SMASHES through the railing. For a moment, the brothers are suspended in air.

Leo undoes his seatbelt automatically and easily opens his door. Allan frantically tries to follow suit but then...

The SUV begins plummeting towards the ocean.

Allan unfastens his seatbelt only to struggle with the door. He desperately pulls on the handle to no avail. It won't budge.

                    LEO
          The lock, undo the lock!

                    ALLAN
          I *did*! I think the door's stuck!

                    LEO
          Follow me, then! Three...

Leo grabs Allan's hand. They're facing the opened passenger-seat door. The SUV is right about to crash into the water.

                    ALLAN
          Leo--

                    LEO
          Two...

                    ALLAN
          I--

                    LEO
          NOW--

CUT TO:


EXT. BEACH PARKING LOT - MORNING

We find Allan and Leo sitting out the back of a parked ambulance, wrapped in blankets and drinking hot cocoa, facing the Pacific Ocean. Allan's SHIVERING violently. Leo looks content.

Emergency responder lights flash and officials chatter in the background.

                    OFFICER (O.S.)
          Your parents will meet you at the
          hospital.

Allan slaps his hand over his eyes. Leo sips his cocoa.

                    ALLAN
          Dude, Dad's gonna kill me for this.

                    LEO
          I'll tell him it was my idea.

ALLAN
That's even worse.

LEO
(chuckles)
I can't believe that worked.

ALLAN
I swear to God, bro, what if we were never actually in a time loop? And I almost killed both of us because I listened to you?

LEO
At least we're alive. We get to move forward and live our lives.

Beat.

ALLAN
Leo?

LEO
Yeah?

ALLAN
What was the craziest loop?

LEO
So, this one time, *I* was behind the wheel, somehow I had convinced you to let me drive, and *you* were dumb enough to let me, and--

FADE OUT.

END.

THE GREEN

(A short radio play)

Written by

Samuel Fordham

Samuel is a Norwich and Cambridge based scriptwriter. His work is primarily science fiction based focusing on human resilience and resourcefulness within harsh and futuristic worlds. Currently, Samuel is working on his own short horror film 'Late Night At The Office', alongside co-hosting feedback workshops and scratch nights.

samfordham45@gmail.com

GROUND CONTROL OPERATIVE: Test flight ready for take off, test subject secure in the capsule.

**SFX: FLICKING OF SWITCHES**

GROUND CONTROL OPERATIVE: And in 5...4...3...2...1.

**SFX: ROCKET TAKING OFF.**

**SFX: RADIO CHATTER, TELEVISION SNIPPETS ABOUT SPACE EXPLORATION.**

**SFX: SPACE ATMOSPHERE – CONTINUOUS THROUGHOUT.**

INT. SPACE CAPSULE – TIME UNKNOWN.

ALBERT WAKES FROM HIS ANESTHESIA. WE HEAR HIM RUSTLE AROUND IN THE CAPSULE.

ALBERT: This is V2 to ground control do you copy?

**SFX: RADIO SILENCE.**

ALBERT: V2 to ground control over?

RADIO SILENCE.

ALBERT: Loss of signal noted, will wait for connection to be re-established. Will note my observations.

ALBERT: Vitals feel normal, heart rate steady.

**SFX: GROANING OF METAL.**

ALBERT: Capsule integrity seems to be holding, rotation slightly towards my left.

ALBERT: It's so dark here.

ALBERT: Getting a view of the curve of the Earth. Still waiting for connection re-establishment.

THE SPACECRAFT TURNS TOWARDS THE EARTH FURTHER. ITS SURFACE IS REVEALED TO HIM. ABSOLUTE JOY, CHILDISH GLEE, EVERYTHING ELSE IS FORGOTTEN.

ALBERT: I can see land! I can see...I don't know what it's actually called.

ALBERT: It's so very green, I've never seen true green like it. And the water too...there is water running through the land! I like it a lot! What is all that brown? And white? What does it feel like? Is it smooth?

ALBERT: Is that where I belong? Is that where you're sending me mission control?

ALBERT: I would love to go to the green it looks so...

ALBERT: It looks so much nicer than behind the bars, no darkness, no harsh white light.

**SFX: GROANING OF METAL.**

ALBERT: I want to breathe the air, the air down there must be so crisp, so fresh.

HE NOTICES THE SUN.

ALBERT: The light, so warm, it is awfully quiet up here.

ALBERT: I'm so alone.

**SFX: GROANING OF METAL.**

ALBERT: Ground control you copy? It's getting hot in here.

**SFX: GROANING OF METAL.**

ALBERT: What's wrong? This doesn't feel right.

ALBERT: Can feel heart rate has gone up.

**SFX: GROANING OF METAL.**

ALBERT: Need water. So much blue.

ALBERT: Ground control please respond.

ALBERT: I think the...it's not safe anymore.

ALBERT: I need air. Want water.

**SFX: GROANING OF METAL.**

ALBERT: Anyone there?

ALBERT: My head feels strange ground control

ALBERT: I think I'm ready to go now.

**SFX: GROANING OF METAL.**

ALBERT: It's getting really quite hot.

ALBERT: I want to get out.

ALBERT: Please want out now.

ALBERT: Head hurt.

ALBERT: Feel tired.

ALBERT: Want home.

**SFX: GROANING OF METAL.**

ALBERT: Want home now.

ALBERT: I sleep.

ALBERT: Home. Need a home. Please.

**SFX: CRASHING OF THE SPACECRAFT AS IT SPEEDS UP.**

ALBERT: Please.

**SFX: CRASHING OF THE SPACECRAFT AS IT SPEEDS UP.**

ALBERT: I was never supposed to be here.

**SFX: EXPLOSION, DEBRIS SCATTERING.**

**SFX: JUNGLE AMBIENCE - ENDS WITH THE CHATTER OF APES.**

END

SORRY FOR YOUR TROUBLE

(An extract from near the beginning
of a feature-length film.)


Written by

Sarah Gamble


After several years of working as a teaching assistant in a secondary school, Sarah had enough writerly inspiration from the ridiculous things that children say and do to quit and pursue a career that pays even less. Her writing explores the various societal roles that women are expected to inhabit and the importance of intergenerational friendships, with a focus on character-driven stories in domestic settings.

sarah.gamble@outlook.com

EXT. MULLIGAN'S PUB - NIGHT

GRACIE sneaks out the back door to savour a moment out of the spotlight.

On a bench a few steps away sits BRIDGET (82), smoking a cigarette. Smartly dressed but clearly exhausted. She nods at Gracie.

> BRIDGET
> Alright, love.

Gracie sits down. Gently leans her head on Bridget's shoulder and closes her eyes for a second.

Beat. Contemplative.

> BRIDGET
> You'd better not be getting tears on my posh jumper. It's cashmere.

> GRACIE
> Since when were you so fancy?

> BRIDGET
> People buy you posh stuff when you're on your way out.

Pause. Bridget finishes her cigarette, and instantly lights another.

> BRIDGET
> How'd it actually happen? Like, what killed him?

> GRACIE
> The head injury.

> BRIDGET
> Right, sure.
>     (pause)
> An ordinary fridge, was it?

> GRACIE
> A fridge-freezer.

> BRIDGET
> Right so. From a window?

GRACIE
Huh?

BRIDGET
Why was someone dropping a fridge-freezer out the window?

GRACIE
No, it was from a delivery van. He was walking past, it fell out... apparently it was very quick.

Bridget snorts.

BRIDGET
Death by fridge. Is that what it said on his death certificate?

Gracie allows herself a laugh.

BRIDGET
I always thought he was an awful prick. Him and his mammy. Both had 'airs'. They stopped going to O'Connor's for their baps when that new M&S in Enniskillen opened. Never knew what you saw in him.

GRACIE
Well, he got me out of this place, so that's something.

BRIDGET
Lucky sod.
     (pause)
Let's go somewhere. Anywhere. Just a wee day trip. Giant's Causeway?

Gracie groans.

BRIDGET
Well there's nowhere else worth going here, is there?

GRACIE
Carrick-a-Rede's a good laugh.

BRIDGET
Never been.

GRACIE
(shocked)
You've never been to Carrick-a-Rede? You've not lived! Seriously, you've lived here your whole life and never been to Carrick-a-Rede? I'll take you. Next time I'm back. Promise.

BRIDGET
Better not leave it too long.

Pause.

BRIDGET
Ach, go on, you're dying to ask me.

GRACIE
You don't have to tell me-

BRIDGET
Six months, maybe a year if I lay off the ciggies. So, six months.

She takes another satisfied puff.

GRACIE
I'm sorry.

Bridget nods again. The closest they can comfortably get to sincerity.

GRACIE
I don't want to go back in.

BRIDGET
There's always some craic to be had. Have you eyed that musician?

GRACIE
What?

BRIDGET
The fella with the tattoos and the nose ring. If I was thirty years younger, he'd be in trouble.

                    GRACIE
          Ach, I'm hardly gonna sneak off from
          me own husband's wake for a quick
          shag, am I?

QUICK CUT TO:


INT. HENDERSON HOUSE, GRACIE'S BEDROOM - NIGHT

GRACIE and JOE are valiantly attempting missionary on the single bed.

Her bedroom hasn't been redecorated since her teens. Posters of various 90s heartthrobs are blue-tacked onto the walls, and a rainbow-coloured dreamcatcher hangs above the bed.

Gracie locks eyes with a poster of Gary Barlow on the wardrobe door.

She looks away quickly.

Sees a TEDDY BEAR sitting on a chair in the corner.

Gracie looks away, and then back.

The Teddy Bear STARES at her.

Gracie squeezes her eyes shut. Joe moans.

                    JOE
          Mmm, that's good. You sure no-one's
          home?

                    GRACIE
          Yeah. The wake's on till nine.

Joe stops thrusting-

                    JOE
          Gosh, that's an awful long wake,
          isn't it? Must've been a popular
          fella. Barry was his name, wasn't
          it?

                    GRACIE
          Kiss me.

A short-lived attempt to shut him up. He kisses her quickly, then-

                    JOE
          Say my name.

                    GRACIE
          I- er-

                    JOE
          Say it-

                    GRACIE
          You didn't tell me what it is.

Joe pauses for a second, then laughs. Kisses Gracie on the forehead. Oddly intimate.

                    JOE
          It's Joe.

He resumes his rhythm-

                    JOE
          What's yours?

                    GRACIE
          Gracie.

Joe stops abruptly, mid-thrust.

                    JOE
          You're Gracie?

                    GRACIE
          Uh-huh.

                    JOE
          Oh- I'm so sorry-

He pulls out and rolls over. Gracie sits up.

                    JOE
          Poor Barry. And the way it
          happened- so awful-

                    GRACIE
          I'd rather not talk about it.

She leaves what she hopes is a dignified pause before leaning in for another kiss, but Joe is staring off into space-

                JOE
I lost my mam when I was four. I don't think I've ever really processed it.

              GRACIE
Oh. That's terrible. I'm sorry.

                JOE
Whatever you need, Gracie, I'm here for you.

He pulls her head onto his chest and starts stroking her hair.

    Gracie is mortified.

              GRACIE
Errr-

                JOE
Sssh. It's okay if you want to cry. I can just hold you. Or I could make you a nice cup of tea?

              GRACIE
Ssh- did you hear that?

                JOE
What?

The sound of a key in a lock. The front door opens.

              GRACIE
Shit! Go out the window-

                JOE
There's no need to be embarrassed about two consenting adults having intercourse-

              GRACIE
Who the fuck says intercourse?

Gracie shoves him out of the bed. We hear the front door shut.

Joe clambers out of the window, only wearing one shoe. Gracie frantically looks for the other.

Footsteps getting closer-

Gracie finds the shoe under her bed, flings it out the window-

The door swings open-

Gracie leaps back into the bed just as her sister GILLIAN (23) barges in. A bit mousy looking, but tough. Their mother's favourite, and doesn't Gracie know it.

                    GILLIAN
    Alright?

                    GRACIE
    Yeah...

Gillian eyes her suspiciously.

                    GILLIAN
    How was it?

                    GRACIE
      (sharp)
    If you were there you'd know.

Gilly ignores this. She moves to the dresser, picks up a tube of mascara.

                    GILLIAN
    Ooh-

She looks in the dresser mirror and applies some mascara.

                    GRACIE
    Can I help you?

                    GILLIAN
    Just popped round to check you're
    not taking a bath with the toaster.

Gillian replaces the mascara and sidles over to the wardrobe. She opens the door and flicks through the clothes on the rail. Brings out a miniskirt, holds it against her thighs.

                    GILLIAN
    Isn't this mine?

                    GRACIE
          Er, I dunno-

                    GILLIAN
          I'm taking it back.

                    GRACIE
          Fine, whatever, are you done?

                    GILLIAN
          Why've you got the window open? It's
          Baltic.

                    GRACIE
          Leave it-

Gillian moves to close it and yelps-

JOE peers through. Looking bashful.

                    JOE
          I think I left my watch.

Gracie reaches onto the bedside table, passes the watch to
Gillian, who passes it to Joe.

                    JOE
          I'm glad our paths crossed, Gracie.
          If only for a short time.

Gillian abruptly shuts the window and pulls the curtains.

                    GRACIE
          Oi!

                    GILLIAN
          What are you thinking? Mammy will
          kill you.

                    GRACIE
          She won't find out.

We hear the front door opening and shutting-

                    IRENE (O.C.)
          Yoo-hoo! Gracie?

                    GRACIE
          Don't tout on me, Gill. Please,
          please, just- don't.

GILLIAN
Fine, relax.
         (pause)
I want that mascara.

GRACIE
Feck off, that's my favourite one-

GILLIAN
Mammy!

GRACIE
Fine, take it, take it- just- don't say anything. Please.


INT. HENDERSON HOUSE, KITCHEN - NIGHT

GRACIE, GILLIAN and IRENE sit around the kitchen table drinking tea. An open Tupperware of homemade Fifteens sits between them.

A heavy silence. Irene slurps her tea.

IRENE
         (nonchalant)
Did I tell you we've a neighbourhood watch WhatsApp group now, Gracie?

GRACIE
Er, no you didn't.

IRENE
Mmm. It's very useful. We can find out who's coming and going.

GRACIE
Seems a bit over the top.

IRENE
Ach, you say that, but if only we'd had it up and running before Mrs

Maguire's garden gnome got defecated.

GRACIE
Defecated?

GILLIAN
D'you mean desecrated, Mammy?

IRENE
I know what I mean. Defecated.

GILLIAN
Someone shat on her garden gnome?

IRENE
Language! But yes, they did.

A pause, as they consider this.

IRENE
So, Gracie. You wouldn't happen to know anything about a young man leaving our house a few minutes before I got back?

GRACIE
Huh?

IRENE
Because Stevie from next door saw him. And said as much on the WhatsApp.

GRACIE
Why aren't you asking Gilly?

IRENE
Because I know your sister would never be so... indiscreet.
        (pause)
Who is he?

GRACIE
A friend.

IRENE
A friend that comes round at night when you're home alone?

GILLIAN
Who's for another?

Gillian gathers the mugs and moves to the kettle. Irene barely notices.

IRENE
(to Gracie)
What line of work is he in?

GRACIE
He's a musician.

IRENE
There's no musicians in Knocklacken. Apart from old Jim the organist.
(pause)
It wasn't Jim, was it?

GRACIE
No!

IRENE
Then who?

Beat, as Irene puts the pieces together...

IRENE
The fella from the wake? Jaysus, Gracie, have you no shame-

GILLIAN
Ach, leave her, ma-

IRENE
The fella with the nose-ring and the-the- nail varnish? What's the matter with you? Barry was a lovely looking fella, but that guy- sure even the tide wouldn't take him out.

Gracie tries to stand up, but Irene grabs her arm. Suddenly angry.

IRENE
You've only been back two days and you've already made a nuisance of yourself. And when you waltz off I'll be left to explain your poor decisions.

GRACIE
Explain to who? Who the fuck cares?

				IRENE
I care!

				GRACIE
Well you shouldn't. My life's no-
one's business but mine.

				IRENE
Now you're being selfish-

				GRACIE
Selfish?

				IRENE
What if you wind up pregnant? You'll
be wanting babysitting from me, I
suppose? Not to mention the money-

				GRACIE
You're overreacting-

				IRENE
Your father would be turning in his
grave to see how you've turned out.
To think of his wee girl sleeping
with half the village and eventually
ending up with a wee bastard in tow-

				GILLIAN
		(loud)
I'm pregnant.

Beat. Gracie and Irene absorb the news in silence.

				GILLIAN
Made it to twelve weeks. It finally
feels real, so...

				IRENE
Ach, love- that's wonderful-

Irene embraces her in a bone-crushing hug.

				GRACIE
		(under her breath)
So it's fine for her to get
pregnant.

                    IRENE
          Because she's married. To an
          architect. Don't you see the
          difference?

Gracie gets up and leaves.

                    IRENE
          Are you not even going to say
          congratulations?

                    GRACIE (O.S.)
              (flat)
          Congratulations.

We hear the front door slam behind her.


EXT. STREET - NIGHT

GRACIE walks quickly. Arms folded, shielding herself from
the rain and wind. She left in such a hurry she didn't take a
coat.

She wipes away a tear with the back of her hand.


EXT. BRIDGET'S HOUSE - NIGHT

GRACIE thundering on the door. BRIDGET opens it, wearing a
nightie.

                    GRACIE
          What are you doing tomorrow?

                    BRIDGET
          I've a snowboarding lesson in the
          morning and then I'm off to Belfast
          for a quickie with Jamie Dornan.

                    GRACIE
          We're getting out of here, Bridget.
          Be ready at seven.

                    BRIDGET
          Ready for what?

Gracie smiles...

THE OPPOSITE OF A HOUSE

(An episode of a television series)

Written by

Wendi Grantham

Wendi Grantham is an actor, singer, and writer. A graduate of Harvard University and the New Actors Workshop, she has acted in stage, film, and television. Her most visible role was that of Shardene Ennis, on HBO's 'The Wire'. She's currently writing a TV series, 'The Opposite of a House.'

wendigrantham@gmail.com

'1980', of the television series 'The Opposite of a House'. Billie (Black, 12), Victor (White, 13), and Jessie (Black, 13) all attend a newly desegregated Junior High school in the suburbs of Wilmington, Delaware. Jessie lives in the city, while Billie and Victor live near the school. Billie and Victor are parents to a doll for a Child Development project, so Billie arranges for Jessie to spend the night, and for them to meet Victor: Billie can hand off the doll, and Victor and Jessie can spend time together, secretly, as it's forbidden. Victor and Jessie go off into the woods together, leaving Billie with Victor's friend, Todd (White, 13). There is no romance between Billie and Todd. They are becoming friends, when, suddenly, things go wrong.

It is May, 1980. *Empire Strikes Back* is in theatres. Todd is not supposed to discuss his ex, Jackie. Billie has just broken the school Triple-jump record.


EXT. TALLEY SCHOOL - DAY

This is the middle of a longer scene. Jessie has just run off with Billie's lower-heeled Candy shoes, and has left her higher heels in the grass near Billie, who is barefoot. The dolls, Prudence, and Donna, sit on the grass, in bassinets. Victor's radio plays. Nina is Jessie's sister; her name is written on a bag in the grass.

                BILLIE
    You make me really want to see
    'Empire' now. It sounds really
    good.

                TODD
    I know! I want to see it again, but
    Victor wants to see *The Shining*.
    Jackie...damnit! Sorry.

                BILLIE
      (talking over him)
    Oh, my Gosh! I read that book! It
    was soo scary! No way I'm seeing
    that! It's okay. You can talk about
    Jackie. I won't say anything.

Todd shakes himself, and refocuses.

                TODD
    Really? Great. I hate horror movies.

                    Victor loves them, of course. I
                    should've never said yes. Jeez.

Beat.

                              BILLIE
                    Were you...together for a long
                    time?

                              TODD
                    Yeah. Two months. She met somebody
                    else. Do you have a boyfriend?

                              BILLIE
                    No. I'm sorry.

                              TODD
                    You don't have to apologize for not
                    having a boyfriend.

                              BILLIE
                    No! Sorry for *you*. Sorry things
                    didn't work out, you know. I
                    just...don't understand any of it.
                    Everybody I know that really seems
                    like they like each other, and then
                    go together? They end up hating each
                    other. Then, that's it? What's the
                    point?

                              TODD
                    Yeah, that's part of it? She doesn't
                    even speak to me anymore. She
                    pretends she doesn't see me. Really?
                    We were, like, good friends, and now
                    I'm invisible. And *she* dumped *me*!
                    If anybody should not be speaking
                    to the other person, it should be
                    me not speaking to her, but no. It's
                    stupid.

                              BILLIE
                    I don't understand girls. They can
                    be so mean. Not that boys can't
                    be, but you know what I mean.
                    It's different. Our other friend,
                    Lindsay...do you know her?

                              TODD
                    JV Basketball manager? I was on JV

for like, 5 minutes. I don't *know
her* know her, but I know who you
mean.

             BILLIE
   She was going out with this guy,
   Mike...do you know Mike Sullivan?

Todd nods no.

             BILLIE
   Oh, good, 'cause I was going to have
   to swear you to secrecy-

             TODD
   I wouldn't say anything. Don't
   worry.

             BILLIE
   I didn't think so, but you have
   to be sure. Anyway, they went out
   for a long time, and they were
   supposed to go to his 8th grade
   prom together, and they picked out
   colors and everything, and, like,
   just this week, she goes, 'Chris
   Albright asked me to 9th grade prom,
   so I'm dumping Mike', and she did!
   It was so awful! Mike is so nice.
   I sat with him after, and he just
   cried in my lap. I felt so bad. He
   kept asking me why, and I didn't
   know why. She didn't say why. She
   just did it. When I asked why, she
   just got all high and mighty about
   it, and said, 'It's a free country,
   right?' Of course it is, but still.
   You know?

             TODD
   Yeah. Wow. Sounds like a power trip.
   People always 'Free country' when
   they power-trip.

             BILLIE
   Yeah! Exactly. But if you're power-
   tripping all the time, then who can
   trust you?

                              TODD
            Exactly.

            You can't build a reputation if you
            can't be trusted.

            Jackie used to do this thing where
            she was, like, super-nice to some
            people, and rude to other people.
            It was like she was two people.
            I didn't...I didn't like that.

            Anyway, I'm cool.

            As long as I stay busy.

He smiles, and then looks off towards the woods for a long
moment. Beat.

                              TODD
            You excited about them painting
            your name on the board? Do you know
            when it is?

                              BILLIE
            I guess. They said next week, before
            the banquet. I mean I am, but
            I think my dad's more excited
            than I am.

                              TODD
            It's a big deal.

                              BILLIE
            I love jumping. 'Specially Triple.
            It's like flying! Wanna see
            something cool?

Billie reaches in the top of her shirt, singles out the track
shoe pendant on a necklace, and holds it up. Todd leans in to
see it.

                              BILLIE
            My dad sent me this when I made
            varsity, but now he's gonna have it
            engraved-

This time, when a car approaches, they are not ready;
it comes so fast, there is nowhere to run.

They quickly separate to a chaste distance; Billie drops the
pendant back inside her shirt, and shifts her position so

she's cross-legged on the ground.

The body of the school is behind them, the circular drive in front of them.

'Magic Carpet Ride', by Steppenwolf, plays loudly, as the car screeches to a halt.

The car has 3 occupants; the one in the backseat, PASSENGER 2, is largely obscured; one bare foot rests where the back passenger window would be if it weren't rolled down. The two white males in the front seats, DRIVER, and PASSENGER 1, in their late teens to early 20s, now openly stare at Billie and Todd; all that separates the passenger car door from them is a sidewalk, which is about four feet across. The driver turns his radio down, but songs can be heard throughout the scene, clashing with those from Victor's transistor radio, which lies in the grass.

> DRIVER
> Whoa-ho! What's this? What's up?

> TODD AND BILLIE
> Hey!

> DRIVER
> How's it going?

> TODD
> It's going pretty good.

> DRIVER
> 'Pretty good', huh?
> (To Billie)
> Is that what you'd say, too? 'Pretty good'?

> BILLIE
> Yeah, I guess so.

> DRIVER
> No fucking way are those babies.

> TODD
> No. It's just...they're just dolls.
> For Human Development.

Billie and Todd attempt to keep this light, but they're scared. This is exactly why they all met behind the school: they didn't want this to happen.

There is a long awkward pause, while the driver and passenger look at Billie and Todd expectantly, as if they are still waiting for answers to their questions. They are smiling, but not with any warmth. Something is wrong.

>                    DRIVER
>           I'm just...confused. Maybe you can
>           help me out. You two seem just as
>           bold as you please talking to us
>           right now, but you're in back of the
>           school, as if you had the good sense
>           to hide whatever the fuck it is
>           you're doing. Do you see how I might
>           be confused? Can you enlighten me?

Billie and Todd are still frozen in place. They smile. A woman's voice calls 'Michael!' in the distance.

>                    PASSENGER 1
>           He's asking you what you're doing
>           back here.

>                    TODD
>           Nothing. We- nothing.

>                    PASSENGER 1
>           Doesn't look like nothing.

>                    DRIVER
>           Looks like something! Looks like

>                    PASSENGER 1
>           She's got her little make-up on, and
>           her little heels, and you've got your
>           hair combed, and your little radio-

>                    DRIVER
>           And two fucking different babies!

>                    TODD
>           One's not-she's only got the one!

The guys in the car laugh, and Todd's face burns with embarrassment, but he keeps smiling.

>                    PASSENGER 1
>           'She's only got the one!' Well, we
>           kinda think that's one too many.
>           What about you? She got the baby by
>           herself?

                    TODD
          I... had Human Development in the
          fall.

                    PASSENGER 1
          Let's see. Give it.

Neither moves.

                    DRIVER
          We're not going to do anything to
          it. Come on, man.

Todd looks at Billie, who doesn't look back, and he picks up
Donna, as she is closer to him, and walks her awkwardly over
to the car, clearly not wanting to get too close.

Passenger 1 takes the doll, stares at Todd, then tosses the
doll up little and catches her.

                    DRIVER
          Whoopseedaisy!

Billie smiles while boys laugh. They are high; the one in the
back seat is lying like he's passed out, as his foot, against
the back passenger window, doesn't move. Between the two in
the front seats, throughout this exchange, they have a joint,
bottled beer, and at least one fifth of Jack Daniels.

                    TODD
               (Trying to fix this)
          We don't really know each other. We
          just have this assignment.

                    DRIVER
          But you want to, is that it? Is that
          why you snuck back here, behind
          the school, where nobody else is,
          because you wanted to 'Know each
          other'?

I asked you a question.

                    TODD
          Not exactly.

                    PASSENGER 1
          What is your name?

                    TODD

Todd.

                    PASSENGER 1

Todd! Finally an answer! You're,
like, the king of non-answers,
Todd.

                    DRIVER

Yeah, Todd, so tell us: what exactly
are you doing, because from here?
It looks like you're trying to make
it with a nigger. And I'll tell you,
Todd: she's pretty. But she's still
a nigger.

                    PASSENGER 1
                    (Laughing)
I'm with Todd on this one, man:
if she's got a pussy, she'll do.
Actually, I'd like to know what a
little black cherry pussy's like,
myself. Is it black on the inside,
too? Is that it, Todd? You wanted
to know what a little black cherry
pussy's like? Say, 'Yes'. Or do you
already know?

                    TODD
                    (reluctantly)
Yes. NO! I mean, I don't-

                    PASSENGER 1

Don't tell me! Tell her. What's your
name? I'm talking to you.

Billie smiles up at the car for a moment, then at Todd, as
if for help, then opens her mouth to answer. Todd's answers,
through the 'Repeating' part of the next exchange, are all
delay.

                    TODD

Her name's Nina.

                    PASSENGER 1

Say, 'Nina...I just want to know...
what your black cherry pussy...
feels like...around my... itty
bitty throbbing ...pink dick!' Say
it!

Todd doesn't look at them, but the threat is clear.

> TODD
> I just

> PASSENGER 1
> Gong! Try again. Say her name! And say it all like you mean it! Smile, too! You gotta lighten up! Humor is important in this life!

> TODD
> Nina.

> PASSENGER 1
> Oh, Nina! Nina!

> DRIVER
> Shut up for a second. That's my grandma's name. Call her something else.

Billie smiles while the two boys in the car pant, and make ape sounds, and laugh.

'Just Want to Be Your Everything' plays softly on Victor's radio, in the background. Todd struggles with every word. Billie stops smiling.

> TODD
> I just want to know what your black cherry pussy feels like

> PASSENGER 1
> Around my itty bitty

> DRIVER
> -Itty bitty or teeny tiny: which one's smaller?

> TODD
> Around my itty bitty

> PASSENGER 1
> Throbbing pink dick

> TODD
> Throbbing pink dick

Todd's face is red, but he tries to smile. The two guys in

the car laugh and laugh.

> DRIVER
> Okay, little monkey: your turn.

> PASSENGER 1
> 'Hot chocolate'!

> DRIVER
> (Laughing) Hot chocolate! Yes! Okay, Hot chocolate: first of all, this is supposed to be fun. You need to be laughing, like we are. Like I said, you gotta have a sense of humor in this life, they say. So, take his hands, look him in the eye, and say, 'Todd...I want you to put your puny pink dick... inside my big black hairy cunt... and make me come ...like this.'

The sounds of female orgasm become gorilla sounds.

HOW MANY MORE JOBS?

(A short film)

Written by

Mazen Haggag

Mazen Haggag is a Half-British, Half-Egyptian scriptwriter that specialises in comedy screenplays that play with other genres. His work is also influenced by the unique cultural experience of his time living between Egypt and the UK and as such, he also explores Muslim representation in his scripts.

mazenmaherhaggag@outlook.com

INT. DINING ROOM, DAY

DAVE (40s) sits at his laptop on his dining table.

He is wearing a wine-red dressing gown and big fluffy slippers. He sips apathetically from his Get Carter mug.

An email pops up on his screen from "jobs@TheSyndicate.org.uk" with the subject "We need you back".

He rolls his eyes, clicks it, skims it and hovers over reply. He stops himself and reports the email as spam.

He blankly stares at the screen before closing his laptop.

Revealed behind it: a crushed punnet of strawberries.

Sadness washes over him as he leaves the room.

CUT TO:


INT. LIVING ROOM, DAY

Dave grimly stares at an empty jar of jam with the TV on in the background.

              TV HOST
     (V.O)
  The world of crime.

Intense music plays. Dave rolls his eyes.

The doorbell rings.

              TV HOST
     (V.O)
  It's dangerous, unpredictable,
  and tough, but is it as tough as
  the law? I'm Ashley Tate, and I'm
  here to show you what happens
  when criminals find themselves
  up against... Britain's Toughest
  Coppers.

Dave begrudgingly moves from his seat as a generic, bad rock music theme song plays.

    CUT TO:

INT/EXT. FRONT DOOR, DAY

The door opens to an overcast day and PAT (40s). He wears a creased suit with no tie and sunglasses.

>DAVE
>Please go away, I'm not coming back.

>PAT
>Dave, I haven't come here lightly. I know you said you were done, but--

Dave shuts the door.

Pat bashes the door.

>DAVE
>WE'RE NOT HAVING THIS CONVERSATION, PAT! I'D ALSO LIKE IT IF YOU STOPPED WHACKING MY NEW DOOR!

The bashing stops.

>PAT
>It's just that the organisation... they'll... uh... they'll kill me.

>DAVE
>The organisation is a few blokes in a garage. If they kill you, they'll be one short of a full pub quiz team.

>PAT
>It's not like that anymore, it's big now. Too big.

>DAVE
>Then why do you need me? Go get some other guy.

>PAT
>Umm, well... Just let me in. I can't speak in the open like this.

Pat nervously looks over his shoulder as if someone else is listening.

>DAVE
>Well, you're doing a pretty good job

                    so far.

Beat.

                         PAT
               Can you just let me in? I'm cold.

Cursing under his breath, Dave opens the door again to see
Pat quickly try to adjust himself to look more professional.

                         DAVE
               Will it make you leave quicker?

                         PAT
               Oh, uhh, yeah.

Dave looks at Pat's desperate face, then closes the door
again.

CUT TO:


INT. KITCHEN, DAY

Dave looks at his strawberries, then to his cooker, adorned
with a small saucepan.

While he scratches his head, Pat tries to squeeze his way in
through an open window.

Suddenly, Pat gets stuck halfway through and screams in pain.
Dave turns over and lets out a deep breath.

                         PAT
               I'm stuck! Awww Dave, I'm in agony!
               Help me! AAAAA--

CUT TO:


INT. DINING ROOM, DAY

Pat stands, scrolling through his phone desperately with one
hand, pressing his injury with the other.

                         PAT
               It's the big one this time Dave,
               you've gotta trust me.

Dave sits down at the table, trying not to fall asleep.

PAT
Aha!

Dave bolts awake. Pat shows him a picture of a dog.

PAT
Isn't she just lovely?

Dave gives a look that could not be more condescending.

PAT
No, you're right, that was unprofessional, what I really wanted to talk about was--

Dave's phone rings.

DAVE
I should take this.

PAT
Oh... go ahead it's all right. Just... Put it on loudspeaker so I know it's not the police or something.

Dave sighs, then answers.

DAVE
Hello?

VOICE ON PHONE (V.O)
Am I speaking to Dave?

DAVE
Yes.

VOICE ON PHONE (V.O)
I'm a representative from The Foundation.

Pat gasps.

Dave's expression sours even more.

                    VOICE ON PHONE
                         (V.O)
                    We're well aware that you've
                    retired, but we've got a big job
                    coming up and we need you.

Pat paces around the room. He begins sweating and
hyperventilating.

                    DAVE
               This is the fifth time you've called
               this week.

                    VOICE ON PHONE
                         (V.O)
                    Sixth, actually. The job we need you
                    for is--

He puts the phone down.

                    DAVE
               See Pat? You're not original or
               unique for doing this, you know
               that?

                    PAT
               Well, uhh... You see--

Pat takes a second to recompose himself.

                    DAVE
               In your own time.

Pat slams his hand on the table. It quivers like jelly.

                    PAT
               I didn't know you were a filthy
               traitor! Working for The
               Foundation? What happened to you?
               If word gets out about this, well...
               unless?

Dave is completely uninterested.

                    PAT
               Unless you did our job, then we
               could keep it, y'know, just between
               me and thee. Our little secret.

                    DAVE
          I am--I mean, I was--always
          freelance. I told you that years
          ago. I worked for them before you
          guys, that's why you hired me.

Beat.

                    PAT
          How are the wife and kids these
          days? It'd be a shame if--

                    DAVE
          Pat, I don't have a wife or kids.

Pat paces around quicker than before. He bites his fist.

                    PAT
          Shit. Uhh, how about this place
          here? It's nice, cozy. It'd be a
          shame if--

                    DAVE
          Pat, please just leave.

                    PAT
          They're gonna be so pissed if I
          don't bring you back with me.

                    DAVE
          How is that my problem?

Pat is on the verge of tears.

                    DAVE
          Aww, Pat, come on, don't do that.
          You can just say I wasn't home.

                    PAT
          They'll just send me back. Unlike
          some of us here, I'm on thin ice.
          This was my big chance to redeem
          myself and you've gone and ruined
          it. I thought we had a real bond, me
          and you.

Dave tries very hard to recall this bond.

                    PAT
          I guess that was all a front then.
          I get it, you're a professional, I'm
          a professional. What we do... isn't
          exactly legal, but I thought there
          was a code. I thought that--

The doorbell rings.

                    DAVE
          Excuse me for a minute.

He leaves before Pat can respond.

CUT TO:


INT./EXT. FRONT DOOR, DAY

Dave opens the front door to find three SUSPICIOUS MEN
(40s-50s) all wearing suits and sunglasses. Behind them is
a POSTMAN (20s) who wears a red polo shirt. He is holding a
parcel with a letter attached to it.

                    SUSPICIOUS MAN 1
          Dave, is it?

                    DAVE
          Bugger off.

Dave ignores the men, squeezes past them, and takes the
parcel.

                    DAVE
          Thank you so much. Have a nice day.

The postman gets into his van and watches the men.

                    SUSPICIOUS MAN 1
          Please sir, I'm with-

                    DAVE
          Bugger. Off. The lot of you.

The postman starts his van and quickly drives off.

                    SUSPICIOUS MAN 1
          You don't understa--

Dave slams the door in their faces.

EXT. FRONT DOOR, DAY

Beat.

          SUSPICIOUS MAN 1
   Who are you guys with?

          SUSPICIOUS MAN 2
   I'm part of The Clan.

The other two men gasp.

          SUSPICIOUS MAN 1
   Jesus Christ, really? I thought
   that was more of an American thing.

CUT TO:

INT. DINING ROOM, DAY

Dave ignores Pat, who is sulking on a chair and opens the letter.

Its message comes in the form of newspaper cuttings. Dave puts on his glasses and reads it dryly.

          DAVE
    (word by word)
   Dave, The Institution has one last
   job for you. Check the parcel. This
   is just a taste of what's to...

He flips the page

          DAVE
 come.

He screws the letter up and throws it away. He looks up to Pat and takes off his glasses.

          DAVE
   Another one? You see that, Pat? It's
   ruining my life!

Pat doesn't respond.

Dave opens the box and his eyes light up. It's full of cash in a zip-lock bag.

DAVE
(rolling eyes)
Oh, here we go.

Pat stands up and starts sarcastically clapping.

PAT
Well, well, well. He finally shows his true colours when money's involved.

DAVE
No, Pat. No. You haven't found my weakness. Stop that you look like a right arse.

Pat freezes.

DAVE
Look at what's under the money Pat.

Pat lifts his head up.

DAVE
You're not gonna see it there. Come closer.

Dave takes the bag of money out of the parcel to reveal a layer of strawberries. Most of them are crushed.

DAVE
I make jam for the village market every week, but some guy from The Syndicate or the bleeding Organisation--

PAT
Actually, that wasn't us. So--

DAVE
Shut the fuck up right now, Pat, I mean it.

Pat obliges and sits back down like a scolded schoolboy.

DAVE
Some people, Organisation notwithstanding, keep infiltrating the post depot every week to slip in a cash offer and ruin my specially ordered, locally sourced carbon fuckin' neutral strawberries! The Post depot, Pat. How much time do these people have? Actually, I know the answer. Too fuckin' much.

Beat.

DAVE
What do you think of all this, Pat? Not as a representative of your "business", but just as Pat? Does this look fair to you?

PAT
You know what? I was actually starting to respect you, I thought you'd really sorted yourself out. But what is this pansy shit? Making jam for the geriatrics?

Dave is done with it. Even more than before.

DAVE
Pansy? Pat, it's not the fucking seventies anymore. Jesus Christ, I shouldn't have let you open your mouth.

He sighs incredibly deeply.

DAVE
Those 'geriatrics' are the only people who have made me feel any emotion in my life. They ask me how I'm doing, they say "good morning" or "lovely to see you" and they give me something to work towards. When Ethel down the road says the jam wasn't quite as good this week, it hurts me. It hurts me more than any powerful crime boss or threat of violence ever could. How am I supposed to make Ethel smile now, Pat? How can I explain it to her?

Dave's heartfelt monologue has penetrated Pat about as well as a circle through a square hole.

                    PAT

        You what?

                    DAVE

        Never mind, just get out of my house.

                    PAT

        I'll tell you what Dave, I've lost the plot here, so... gimme some of your jam.

Finally, Dave is caught by surprise.

                    DAVE

        What?

                    PAT

        You heard me. If it's any good, I'll get out and pretend none of this ever happened.

                    DAVE

        And if it's not?

Beat.

                    PAT

        I dunno... I'll hit you in the gut or something?

                    DAVE

        Deal.

CUT TO:


INT. KITCHEN, DAY

The jar is refilled with jam. Dave gets some on a spoon.

                    PAT

        What, not even a slice of toast?

                    DAVE
          Just try it before I rip your mouth
          off.

Pat takes the spoon and goes for it.

He tastes it. He moves it all over his mouth.

Suddenly... He gets it.

He smiles as if it was the first time he's ever felt happy.

                    PAT
          Tell Ethel she can shove it where
          the sun don't shine. This--this is
          beautiful.

Pat makes his way to the front door.

                    PAT
          Deal's a deal Dave, I'll leave.
          I take it back. I do respect you...
          mate.

Dave is slightly flattered, but mostly relieved to get rid of Pat.

CUT TO:


EXT. FRONT DOOR, DAY

The three men are still standing at the door.

                    SUSPICIOUS MAN 3
          So, as I was saying, The
          Conglomerate-

Pat bursts through the door and brushes past them, but before he leaves, he turns back around.

                    PAT
          Don't bother him lads, just try his
          jam. It's something else.

Pat walks off into the horizon, as if he has achieved something. The suspicious men watch on, confused.

CUT TO:

INT. LIVING ROOM, DAY

Dave sits in the living room with his jam.

                    TV HOST
It's cases like these that show that even in the world of Britain's Toughest Coppers, maybe a few crooks can be redeemed.

He dips his finger in and tries it. A glowing grin melts over his face.

End.

LOVE LIFE ADVICE LINE

A radio drama


Written by

Ava Hamilton












Ava Hamilton's screenwriting work mainly focuses on the
trials and tribulations of friendship and family dynamics
which occur in everyday life. Recent works consist of a
comedy series depicting grief within young people and a
film, The Worst Half, which takes place at a wedding and
explores themes of romance, secrecy, and sisterhood.

Avaeuphemia02@gmail.com

**SFX: SCRATCHY DIAL TONE.**

AUTOMATED VOICE — Hello and thank you for calling The Love Life Advice Line. Our expert call handlers strive to provide the best advice for our customers. Please remember that all calls are anonymous, but they are recorded for research and training purposes. Thank you.

**SFX: THE PHONE DIALING AND CONNECTING.**

CALL HANDLER — Hello and welcome to Love Life Advice Line. Thank you for using our service. How can I assist you today?

MALE CUSTOMER — Can I just ask a question before we begin?

CALL HANDLER — Of course, our top priority is ensuring that our customers feel comfortable during our calls.

MALE CUSTOMER — How many experts does your company have?

CALL HANDLER — There are over five hundred of us in our UK branch.

MALE CUSTOMER — And you won't judge me, will you?

CALL HANDLER — No sir, this is a safe space. Here at Love Life Advice Line we care about our customers.

MALE CUSTOMER — Because if you do, I'll know.

CALL HANDLER — Just like your identity is kept anonymous, so is mine.

MALE CUSTOMER — Right, okay.... So... is this when I tell you, my problem?

CALL HANDLER — That is correct.

MALE CUSTOMER — So, I just say it, out loud, now?

CALL HANDLER — Take your time, sir. But please bear in mind you are charged nineteen pence per minute.

MALE CUSTOMER  Nineteen? On your website it says sixteen! That's false advertisement, that's a criminal offence!

CALL HANDLER  Our website hasn't been updated for five years and you may terminate the call at any moment during this conversation. Now, how may I help you?

MALE CUSTOMER  I think my wife and I are having issues. Or more like, she's an issue.

**SFX: THE SOUND OF TYPING ON A KEYBOARD.**

MALE CUSTOMER  What are you writing down? I thought this was anonymous!

CALL HANDLER  I'm taking notes on the situation.

MALE CUSTOMER  Right, I see.

CALL HANDLER  Can you expand on this statement?

MALE CUSTOMER  She seems more distant than usual.

CALL HANDLER  In what capacity?

MALE CUSTOMER  She's less talkative. And she hasn't cooked me my favourite dinner in a while. I'm gluten free so good meals are hard to come by. It's an affair, isn't it?

CALL HANDLER  Here at Love Life Advice Line we try to have a more positive outlook on a situation. An affair seems like a rather big assumption.

**SFX: LEAVES RUSTLING AS A BIRD TAKES OFF.**

CALL HANDLER  Sir, where are you?

MALE CUSTOMER  I'm in the garden shed. I don't want her to see me.

| | |
|---|---|
| CALL HANDLER | I see. Is your hiding a result of the shame you feel for having this conversation? |
| MALE CUSTOMER | You're judging me! I have done nothing wrong. You think I'm guilty! |
| CALL HANDLER | I'm on no one's side here sir, but marriage is a two-way street. On reflection, do you recall letting your wife down in anyway? |
| MALE CUSTOMER | I was ten minutes late picking her up from the hairdressers the other day. |
| CALL HANDLER | Was it raining? |
| MALE CUSTOMER | There wasn't a cloud in the sky. |

**SFX: MORE TYPING ON A KEYBOARD.**

| | |
|---|---|
| CALL HANDLER | I see. How long have you been married? |
| MALE CUSTOMER | Twenty-five years. We celebrated in April. |
| CALL HANDLER | Congratulations. That's a remarkable commitment. |
| MALE CUSTOMER | I took her out for fish and chips. We walked along the pier where we met. |
| CALL HANDLER | That sounds very romantic. |
| MALE CUSTOMER | That's what I thought! We held hands, I gave her half my fish cake. |
| CALL HANDLER | Generosity is a great way to make your partner feel valued. |

**SFX: TYPING ON KEYBOARD.**

| | |
|---|---|
| CALL HANDLER | How else are you keeping the romance alive? |
| MALE CUSTOMER | I keep the grass in good shape. I always make the bed. I put the toilet seat down. |

CALL HANDLER   Making your wife's day easier is a great way to show her you care. Does anything else come to mind?

MALE CUSTOMER   I heat up the car before she gets in it. I listen to her talk about her day. I change the bins.

CALL HANDLER   Have you not completed any of these acts of love recently?

MALE CUSTOMER   I never forget. But the other day when I brought her daily cup of tea she left it untouched.

CALL HANDLER   Was the milk spoiled?

MALE CUSTOMER   No.

CALL HANDLER   Was it brewed to the right strength?

MALE CUSTOMER   I know the colour better than myself.

CALL HANDLER   Was there something wrong with the mug?

**SFX: SILENCE ON THE LINE. THEN THE DISTANT SOUND OF BIRDS CHIRPING.**

CALL HANDLER   Sir, are you still here?

MALE CUSTOMER   Yes, I'm here.

CALL HANDLER   Did you hear me, was there something wrong with the mug?

MALE CUSTOMER   A mug is a mug. Let's not fuss about it.

**SFX: TYPING FOR AN UNCOMFORTABLY LONG TIME.**

CALL HANDLER   Sir, I can only help you if you allow me to.

MALE CUSTOMER   I can feel you judging me through the phone!

CALL HANDLER   I assure you I am not. Please, continue.

MALE CUSTOMER   Well...I was unloading the dishwasher the other day...

CALL HANDLER	Sharing chores is an important element for a healthy and stable relationship.

MALE CUSTOMER	Yes...

CALL HANDLER	Remember sir, please do not withhold valuable information.

MALE CUSTOMER	I got too confident, I tried to carry more than I could handle. I dropped a mug, it smashed.

CALL HANDLER	The world is an imperfect place. Accidents happen all the time.

MALE CUSTOMER	I feel terrible.

CALL HANDLER	That's natural. How did your wife react?

MALE CUSTOMER	It happened when our daughter came to visit. I told my wife it was her.

**SFX: FRANTIC TYPING ON KEYBOARD**

CALL HANDLER	Firstly sir, lying is never the right solution. It can cause intimacy issues as it breaks bonds of trust. Secondly, one must never involve their children in marital problems as this can cause animosity not only between spouses but also between parent and child. Was there a reason why you lied?

MALE CUSTOMER	It was her favourite mug.

**SFX: FRANTIC, HELLBENT TYPING ON KEYBOARD.**

CALL HANDLER	And what made this particular mug so special?

MALE CUSTOMER	Her Mum bought it for her from John Lewis. I tried to find a new one on their website but it was a collector's item, limited edition. You see, my wife she's ladybird fanatic. The mug had a *sospita vigintiguttata* ladybird on it

**SFX: SILENCE ON THE LINE**

CALL HANDLER   Dad? That was you!

**SFX: THE ABRUPT DISCONNECT TONE.**

AUTOMATED VOICE   Thank you for using Love Life Advice Line. We hope our experts have led you to a positive conclusion. Please remember that your identity is protected as all calls are anonymous. Our team wishes you the best in your relationship.

LOST FOR WORDS

(A complete short comedy radio play.)

Written by

Phoebe Haywood

Phoebe Haywood is a scriptwriter primarily for radio, with experience in live comedy production, both at the Edinburgh Fringe and from the radio show she presents. Most of her work is comedic, with whimsical or fantastical elements. As an ADHD writer, she uses humour to represent, express, and explore neurodivergence.

All details in square brackets deliberately left unspecified to allow flexible choices in production.

pg@phoebeg.com

DAVID
(V.O.)
Ever gone into a room and then forgotten why?

You had an idea of what you were doing, what you wanted. Then you entered the room and — POOF! Suddenly you don't have a reason for being there, can't even think of one.

Now imagine that with talking.

**SFX: BACKGROUND HUBBUB OF RESTAURANT — CHATTER, CUTLERY SCRAPING ON PLATES, GLASSES CLINKING.**

DAVID
I might have the salad. Or maybe the cheeseburger? No, I'll go for the salad —

**SFX: FOOTSTEPS APPROACH.**

WAITER
Hi, what can I get for you?

DAVID
Oh. Uh.

**SFX: BACKGROUND HUBBUB FADES OUT.**

(V.O.)
See, I've got ADHD and words can be hard for me.

I think faster than I can talk. So when I do speak, I have to slow myself down. And sometimes... my mouth just can't keep up with my brain. That's when I can't say anything at all.

Because when something like THIS happens, what's going on inside and out is a bit different:

**SFX: BACKGROUND HUBBUB RETURNS.**

WAITER
Sir? What can I get you?

                    DAVID
Uh.

> **MUSIC:'SPRING' BY VIVALDI REPLACES SFX HUBBUB.**

There's a waiter. I need to order. I have to make a choice. But I had a choice. What was the choice? I couldn't decide. Between salad and cheeseburger.

> **SFX: BACKGROUND HUBBUB REPLACES 'SPRING' MUSIC.**

I wanted... I — Hm.

> **MUSIC:'SPRING' BY VIVALDI REPLACES SFX HUBBUB.**

Why did I choose one over the other? I can't remember. So I can't choose now. Because I don't remember what I chose then. Wow, that's a lot of menu options. Is that the Comic Sans font?

> **SFX: BACKGROUND HUBBUB REPLACES 'SPRING' MUSIC.**

I — I'd like...

                    MIRANDA
I think you said you'd like the salad. Why don't I order first, so you can take a minute, honey?

> **SFX: BACKGROUND HUBBUB FADES OUT.**

                    DAVID
                    (V.O.)
In these moments, I just need time to sort out my own thoughts. Miranda knows this and she always gives me that time. Sometimes she steps in like this to make sure others do too. She's wonderful. My girlfriend is wonderful.

I'm going to marry her.

> SFX: ENGINE — WHICH THEN QUIETENS AS CAR DRAWS TO STOP. CAR BOOT OPENS — SUITCASE PUT IN — BOOT SHUTS. PASSENGER DOOR OPENS — MAN GETS IN — DOOR SHUTS. ENGINE GETS LOUDER AS CAR DRIVES OFF.

MARK
Hey David, thanks again for picking me up. God, that train journey took for ever —

DAVID
I'm going to marry Miranda.

MARK
Woah. Seriously? Oh wow. Wow! Congrats, man! That's great! I mean, you've been together — what, three, four years? Have you asked her yet, or did you just decide...?

DAVID
I've got us tickets to [MUSIC FESTIVAL] and I'm going to ask her at the festival.

MARK
Didn't you guys first meet each other there?

DAVID
Yep. We met there during [SONG] by [BAND] — before they split up. But they're doing a reunion tour this year, appearing at [FESTIVAL] again. So...

MARK
You're gonna ask her during the song! Man, that's so romantic. It sickens me.

DAVID
Thanks, Mark.

MARK
Wait. Is this why you invited me all the way down from bloody Scotland to visit?

DAVID
Of course. Can you come film the proposal for me?

MARK
I'd better be your best man for this.

DAVID
Duh. Now, I've got tickets for me, Miranda, you, and Kate —

MARK
Who's Kate again?

DAVID
Miranda's sister. Figured she should be there too.

MARK
Fair enough. Got a speech for it?

DAVID
Yeah, I want to do it properly. Down on one knee, holding up the ring, declaring my love...

MARK
You're such a romantic sap, David. I bet your favourite movie is the Notebook.

DAVID
And?

**SFX: CAR ENGINE FADES OUT.**

(V.O.)
The phrase "lost for words" doesn't really apply. I do have the words, they're inside my head. There's just too many of them to say. So I can't say anything in the end.

It's not a huge problem because I can usually manage. I don't normally have so many thoughts that they jam up my speech.

Unless I'm under sudden or extreme pressure. Then my brain goes into overdrive.

**MUSIC: [DIFFERENT SONG] BY [BAND] — ALREADY HALFWAY THROUGH.**

MIRANDA
I can't believe you got us tickets to this, David! It's amazing — you're amazing!

DAVID
I'm just glad you like it. We met at this stage, do you remember —

MIRANDA
Of course I do. And this band was playing! This is so special, David. It's like we're falling in love all over again.

KATE
Hey sis, come here. I'll take a pic of you two lovebirds.

MARK
No need, Kate, I'm already filming.

KATE
Really? Why?

MARK
No reason. Shut up.

**MUSIC: [DIFFERENT SONG] ENDS — [MENTIONED SONG] STARTS.**

MIRANDA
Oh my God. It's our song! David, our song!

DAVID
Hey, Miranda... I wanted to ask you something.

MIRANDA
Yeah?

DAVID
I —

**SFX: CLOWN NOSE HONK. ALL MUSIC PAUSES — SILENCE.**

          (*V.O.*)

I think, in other circumstances, I'd be all right. Of course proposing is tense and nerve-wracking. But I love Miranda and I'm a hundred per cent certain I want to marry her. The only catch: I have so many things I want to say to her in my proposal. I wrote three A4 pages before Mark helped me edit it down.

Now, I've practised it and practised it — so theoretically I should still remember it even when I'm nervous.

          **SFX: CLOWN NOSE HONKS AGAIN.**

I'm not nervous. I'm terrified.

That is a real clown that's just appeared — there, past Miranda's shoulder, in full clown outfit and handing out balloon animals.

I hate clowns. It's not quite a phobia, but it's borderline. So now I'm definitely on edge.

And my brain is racing faster than Formula One.

          **MUSIC: [SONG].**

          MIRANDA

Yes, David?

          DAVID

I — Aha. Um.

          **MUSIC: 'ENTRY OF THE GLADIATORS' BY JULIUS FUČÍK (FAMOUSLY ASSOCIATED WITH CIRCUS RING MUSIC).**

Clown. That's a clown. Why is there a clown at a music festival? Is it for the kids here? Why do kids like clowns? They're so creepy. Why does no one remember the 2016 clown scare apart from me? That was awful. They all had knives. Knives!

**MUSIC: [SONG].**

MIRANDA

David? Are you all right?

MARK

(*sotto voce*)

C'mon man. You got this.

KATE

(*also sotto voce, but less subtle*)

Oh! Is this what this is?! Oh my God!

DAVID

Uhhhhhhh —

**MUSIC: 'ENTRY OF THE GLADIATORS'.**

Wait, everyone is looking at me. Miranda's looking at me. Miranda. I had something I was doing with Miranda. I needed to do something. To... ask her. Something. MARRY! Oh God, I need to propose. What do I say? "Will you marry me —" No! That's at the end. Other things to say first. What were they? "When we met —" No. "You are the light —" No. Come on, David, you know this. You wrote this. You used Grammarly. Oh my God, that clown is staring at me. What the hell is that shoe size?

**MUSIC: [SONG].**

MARK

Uh oh.

KATE

What's wrong?

MARK

Clown. Three o'clock.

KATE

Oh, cool.

MIRANDA

No, not cool. David hates clowns.

I think it's really stressing him
out. Hey, David? Honey? Do you want
to go somewhere else?

              DAVID
No! No, we have to — It's —

         **MUSIC: 'ENTRY OF THE GLADIATORS'.**

Go somewhere else? No. No. No. We
can't do that. We have to be here.
Why though? Why here? Oh, the band.
The BAND! I need to propose during
our song. It's a reunion tour. Back
at [FESTIVAL]. This is my only
chance! But. Words. To propose.
Engagement. Ring. What was I meant
to say? What was I trying to say?
WHAT DO I SAY RIGHT NOW?!

              **MUSIC: [SONG].**

              MIRANDA
OK, be real with me, Mark. Is this
what I think it is?

              MARK
Um. Yeah.

              MIRANDA
All right. That's — You should
probably stop filming. I don't
think he wants this bit on camera.

              DAVID
I just need to — to tell you
something, Miranda. It's — MMMM —

              MIRANDA
Kate, can you grab me some food from
one of the stalls? I think his blood
sugar has dropped.

              KATE
His blood sugar?

              MIRANDA
He finds it hard to process things
when it's low. It's a thing. And
Mark, can you go with Kate? It's her
first time at [FESTIVAL].

							MARK

Sure thing.

				**SFX: RECEDING FOOTSTEPS.**

							DAVID

MMM — MMM —

							MIRANDA

OK, David, I can tell that you're not processing things well right now. Your eyes are doing that thing where they flick around side to side, and you've started making noises instead of words. Let's sit over here. Come on.

				**SFX: THEY WALK TO THE SIDE AND SIT.[SONG] GROWS FAINTER.**

It's quieter here. Just take a minute.

							DAVID

No, but — I'm sorry. The music.

							MIRANDA

I don't care. Here, have a sip of this. That'll tide you over for now.

				**SFX: CAN LID SNAPS. DRINK FIZZES. SLURPING.**

							DAVID

But — it was our song. I didn't want to — to take you away from that.

							MIRANDA

I told you, I don't care. I just care about you. That you're OK. It's not our song if we're not both enjoying it.

							DAVID

I — I love you.

							MIRANDA

I love you too.

				**MUSIC: [SONG] FADES OUT ENTIRELY.**

DAVID
(*V.O.*)
Those are the only words I ever really needed to say, aren't they? Looking into her eyes, feeling how I felt about her, knowing I want to marry her — and just saying: "I love you".

And of course:

**MUSIC: [SONG] RETURNS, STILL FAINT.**

Miranda. Will you marry me?

MIRANDA
Yes, David. I will.

**MUSIC: [SONG] FADES OUT AGAIN BRIEFLY —**

DAVID
(*V.O.*)
Besides, I can always say those things I wanted to say to her during our wedding vows. And this time, I'll bloody well take the script with me.

**MUSIC: 'ENTRY OF THE GLADIATORS' RETURNS — LOUD AND TRIUMPHANT.**

AN AMERICAN IS A CREATURE
OF FOUR WHEELS

(A short play)


Written by

Rosie Johns










Rosie Johns is a writer from Ipswich, who completed her bachelor's in Film and Television Studies at UEA, before starting her Masters in Scriptwriting. Her writing examines political themes through character driven narratives. Alongside her studies, she has written a docu-series for BBC Sounds and contributes to independent writing magazines.

rosemaryjohns00@gmail.com

*An American flag is hanging on the back wall of the space.*

*There is a table with a tape recorder. A box file. A chair.*

*Sat on the chair is ANARA*

*She presses PLAY on the tape recorder.*

                    TAPE RECORDER
You will be asked a series of questions. To begin you will be asked to raise your right hand.

*(Anara raises her right hand.)*

                    TAPE RECORDER
I hereby declare, on oath, that I absolutely and entirely renounce and abjure all allegiance and fidelity to any foreign prince, potentate, state, or sovereignty, of whom or which I have heretofore been a subject or citizen; that I will support and defend the Constitution and laws of the United States of America, so help me God.

                    ANARA
I hereby declare, on oath, that I absolutely /and entirely …

                    TAPE RECORDER
Do you promise to tell the truth, the whole truth and nothing but the truth?

                    ANARA
Yes.

*(She lowers her right hand.)*

                    TAPE RECORDER
At this point, the officer will ask for your Green Card and passport, and then take a photo and fingerprints.

*(Anara gives an exaggerated smile for an imaginary camera)*

TAPE RECORDER
What is your name?

ANARA
Anara.

TAPE RECORDER
What is your country of origin?
Country of nationality?

ANARA
America. I was born here.

TAPE RECORDER
Are or were your parents American
Citizens?

ANARA
Yes, they are. They answered the
questions right.

TAPE RECORDER
Have you ever been declared legally
incompetent or confined to a mental
institution?

ANARA
No. They studied a lot to pass. My
mother forgot the answers straight
away, but my father still practises.

TAPE RECORDER
Who makes federal laws?

ANARA
Congress. As if Border Control will
knock at any time.

TAPE RECORDER
What ocean is on the west coast of
the United States?

ANARA
The Pacific Ocean. But, he loves
it, he thinks the more he knows, the
more American he becomes.

TAPE RECORDER
What do we call the first 10
amendments to the Constitution?

ANARA
The Bill of Rights. My mother, less
so.

*(Anara lifts the box file from the table on to her lap and looks through it)*

TAPE RECORDER
Have you ever served in a military
unit? Paramilitary unit? Police
unit? Self-defence unit? Vigilante
unit? Rebel group? Guerilla group?
Militia? Insurgent organisation?

ANARA
Here's what they needed.

*(Anara pulls out a mini American Flag on a mini flag stand, which she sets on the table)*

ANARA
You only get that when you pass the
test.

TAPE RECORDER
Have you ever been a habitual
drunkard?

*(Anara pulls out a cassette case and gestures to the player)*

ANARA
This, and

*(Anara sets down the cassette case, pulls out a pile of papers and clears her throat.)*

TAPE RECORDER
What does habitual drunkard mean?

*(She reads from the paper.)*

ANARA
Here are the key objectives of this
lesson.

TAPE RECORDER
Have you ever advocated, either
directly or indirectly, for the
overthrow of any government by
force or violence?

                    ANARA
You will promise to completely
give up all loyalty to leaders and
governments of other countries
where you were a / subject or
citizen before.

                    TAPE RECORDER
What is freedom of religion?

                    ANARA
You will promise that your loyalty
is to the United States only. You
will promise to use a weapon if the
U.S. government asks you to.

                    TAPE RECORDER
What was one important thing that /
Abraham Lincoln did?

                    ANARA
You will promise, before God, all
this without influence from anyone
or hesitation.

*(Anara discards the paper to the floor and sets the box file down)*

                    TAPE RECORDER
Why does the flag have 50 stars?

                    ANARA
50 states.

                    TAPE RECORDER
Do you now have, or did you ever
have, a hereditary title or an order
of nobility in any foreign country?

                    ANARA
Ha.

                    TAPE RECORDER
What does hereditary mean?

                    ANARA
Hereditary, like, I got my mother's
eyes.

TAPE RECORDER
Have you ever used a weapon or threatened to use a weapon against anyone?

ANARA
She was picking gravel out of my hands one morning on the walk to school, said, I named you after pomegranates, they leave red on your hands just like this, just like falling over.

TAPE RECORDER
Name one state that borders Canada.

ANARA
New Hampshire. I asked my grandma why my mother would name me after bloody hands and she said that I must truly be an American to take something beautiful, rip it apart and blame it for having blood.

TAPE RECORDER
In what year was the Constitution written?

ANARA
Seventeen something… I don't need to get it right; I was born here.

TAPE RECORDER
Do you file your taxes every year?

ANARA
 My grandma said, Anara, why is it always hands that are bloody? You must ask yourself- where is the blood coming from?

TAPE RECORDER
Have you ever married someone to gain an immigration benefit?

ANARA
No.

TAPE RECORDER
Have you ever persecuted anyone

because of race, religion or
national origin?

ANARA
No, but my father went alone to
every yankees game, wore a yankees
hat bought hot dogs giant foam
fingers sang star spangled banner
got called a terrorist on the
subway. He laughed and told me that
being American means you have nine
lives and a big big mouth.

TAPE RECORDER
Have you ever helped anyone to enter
the U.S. illegally?

ANARA
He drove to the stadium after that.
Said real Americans have four
wheels.

TAPE RECORDER
Where do you currently live?

ANARA
In Washington. If I could live
anywhere I'd choose a big empty room
and I'd sleep on the floor.

TAPE RECORDER
Have you ever claimed to be a U.S.
citizen?

ANARA
My grandma said that I'm not
American, I just live here / but
I've never not been here, I've
always lived in America, and so will
my children and their children, and
theirs after that.

TAPE RECORDER
Have you ever failed to support your
dependents?

ANARA
My mother explained to me that they
had to move because their home had
become too tangled up, like the

knots in my hair after swimming, or the roots of the trees in the forest.

TAPE RECORDER
When did you move to the United States?

ANARA
In 1991 my parents came to New York,

TAPE RECORDER
Name one war fought by the United States in the 1900s.

ANARA
In 1991 America bombed the only baby formula factory in Iraq. Colin Powell said it was a biological weapons facility but when they sent investigators into the basement all they could find were cans of powdered milk and a one inch thick layer of

melted

human

fat.

TAPE RECORDER
If the law requires it, are you willing to bear arms on behalf of the U.S.?

ANARA
You have to remind yourself, that this is what Americans do. We burn ants with magnifying glasses, set alight tiny homes from all the way up here and look- they disappear just like that! Do you want to try? How many can you get?

TAPE RECORDER
How many trips have you taken outside the U.S. in the past five years?

ANARA

I heard my mother tell my grandma that she wished they didn't have to pick between the home with overgrown roots and the home with the axe.

TAPE RECORDER
Have you ever lied to gain public benefits?

ANARA
When I was younger I told her she must really love cooking because that's all she ever does. She went upstairs for the rest of the day and my dad had to order us a pizza for dinner.

TAPE RECORDER
Have you ever worked in a prison or jail? Prison camp? Labour camp? Any place where people are forced to stay?

ANARA
She used to be a teacher. There's an endless hissing that follows her, like water in a pan of hot oil.

TAPE RECORDER
Have you ever been involved in genocide? Torture? Killing someone? Badly hurting someone? Not letting someone practise their religion?

ANARA
I file my taxes every year.

TAPE RECORDER
Have you ever sold or given weapons to anyone?

ANARA
Have you?

TAPE RECORDER
Do you understand the full Oath of Allegiance to the U.S.?

ANARA
Who killed the ants- me, or the magnifying glass?

TAPE RECORDER
What is the Oath of Allegiance?

ANARA
Do you hereby declare, on oath, that you will always keep at least a one inch thick layer of melted human fat between you and your home country, that you will have a big big mouth nine lives four wheels use a weapon when asked and spit pomegranate blood when you speak,

So help me God?

THE SOUNDS OF ANXIETY


Written by

Yavuz Orhun Kilic










Yavuz Orhun Kilic (Y.O.K.) is a Turkish writer for comics, tv, movies, plays and videogames. He is currently working on his comic book series "Universe 7777", an existential piece that questions the existence of God, the objectivity of our reality and the possibility of alternate universes. His writing blends genres of science fiction, horror, and fantasy to create a unique voice all his own. His work features a broad and colourful cast of characters with unique motivations and viewpoints that often delve into moral ambiguity.

+44 7469 043529
orhunk99@gmail.com

**The Cast of Characters**

Alex, 25 years old, musician
Anx, 25 years old, personification of anxiety


**ACT 1**
**Scene 1**

Alex's living room at night. There is a sofa and a table in the scene. Behind the table, a guitar is hidden from the audience. On the floor, crumpled papers are visible. Music plays. It is a Turkish song ("Mor ve Ötesi-Cambaz"). ALEX (25) sits on the sofa and writes something in her notebook. She rips off the page and crumples it before throwing it on the floor. ANX (25) enters. The music stops. Anx begins to play with the papers on the floor like a child.

Alex sees Anx and lets out a sigh before continuing to write.

                ANX
Hi!

Alex ignores her, staring down at the page she was working on.

                ANX
             (CONT'D)
Ugh, I said "Hi!".

                ALEX
I heard you the first time, now get lost!

                ANX
Ugh, come on! Didn't you miss me?

                ALEX
You were here last night too, and the day before, and before that. How could I possibly miss you?

                ANX
Because I am your guardian! The biggest guide in your life! Maybe even… the friend you always wanted?

ALEX
None of the above... Now seriously,
fuck off. I'm busy.

Anx sits down next to Alex, attempting to peek at her papers.
Alex keeps them close to her chest.

ANX
What are you up to anyway? Is it
related to that crappy music you
were listening to?

Alex turns her face towards Anx. Anx smiles back at her.

ALEX
First, it is not crappy. Second,
you're the one who recommended that
song to me in the first place!

ANX
Oh yeah! The Turkish one. Nice, but
I also told you to buy a new charger
for the laptop. Are you so lazy
that you're just gonna write it in a
notebook?

Alex stops looking at her, embarrassed.

ALEX
If I had money...

ANX
I did warn you, didn't I? Being a
musician requires some talent which
you don't particularly have. I hope
we don't end up living in a box.

ALEX
We won't! Just shut up! I've got a
real chance to impress them here,
and you're killing my flow. Now
please, shut up already.

**ACT 2**
**Scene 2**

A Beat. Anx plays with her own hair, sprawled out slightly on the floor. Alex continues writing. They are still in the same room.

ANX
You're gonna be on stage, right?

ALEX
Yes...

ANX
Remember to go to the bathroom! I don't want you pissing yourself on stage.

Alex drops the pen, staring at Anx.

ALEX
What? Why would I piss myself?

ANX
Well, considering the amount of beer you drink…

ALEX
Just stop talking already. Besides, I'm not drinking before I go up.

ANX
What if you come across a good-looking dude?

ALEX
Not happening.

ANX
Which part? Your chances of coming across a good- looking dude, or having a beer with him?

ALEX
Right, from now on, I'm just focusing on my work.

Alex grabs her notebook and stands up, circling the sofa while Anx follows.

ALEX
Stop following me!

ANX
This reminds me of something. Be careful with people in the crowds.

Alex stops running and turns her face back to Anx who waves at her.

ALEX
Why?

ANX
Well, I remember hearing about some guy who got shot at a bar while playing music. He was Turkish as well.

ALEX
I don't remember that. You're lying.

ANX
No, you remember too. A customer in a bar asked for a song and Turkish singer said "no". Afterwards...

Anx pretends she holds a gun in her hand, pulling the imaginary trigger and mimicking her head exploding.

ALEX
You're not funny, you know that right? Besides, I'm not scared.

ANX
I'm not trying to scare you; I'm just protecting you.

Alex sits on the sofa, taking out her guitar beside it and checking the chords. Anx sits on the table this time.

ALEX
Well, you're not helping...

> ANX
> What am I doing then?

> ALEX
> You're annoying me, ok? I try to ignore you as much as my mind allows me, you will pass away eventually… Wait, that's a good line, I'm stealing that.

**ACT 3**
**Scene 3**

Alex takes her notes and starts to sing a song with her guitar. Anx listens to her carefully. The lights are on Alex. (The same scene)

> ALEX
> (Singing)
> "Good days will come, just wait.... it will be gone, just say 'it will pass eventually'"

Anx claps. Alex takes notes.

> ANX
> Wow! That was… A pile of shit! What the hell was that?

> ALEX
> I told you I'm ignoring you!

> ANX
> Oh yeah? It doesn't sound like that...

Anx takes the guitar and puts it on the floor, sitting down close to Alex. Alex instinctively puts her fingers in her ears.

> ANX (CONT'D)
> Deep down, you know you're just a shitty artist... Not creative enough, not talented enough. No matter what you do to improve

                    yourself, it's just a waste of time.

Anx hugs Alex very tightly. Alex cannot breathe. Trying to push Anx away.

                         ALEX
                      (choking)
                    Anx, I can't breathe! Let me go!

                         ANX
                    Although you have so many flaws, I
                    won't stop loving you.

                         ALEX
                    Stop! I said stop!

Anx releases Alex, sitting at the opposite side of the couch with her head turned away.

                         ALEX(CONT'D)
                    This is not love Anx.. This is
                    basically the opposite of love.

                         ANX
                    This is my way of loving you.

                         ALEX
                    I don't care! Why can't you just be
                    a little more positive? All you do
                    is smother me and tell me I suck.

Anx turns her face towards Alex.

                         ANX
                    Sorry, it doesn't work like that.
                    If you wanna get rid of me, it's
                    totally okay. Start taking your
                    magical pills now!

                         ALEX
                    It's called medication, and I'm
                    not taking it again. Look, I don't
                    hate you. You've done a lot for me,
                    inspired me. Without you, I can't do
                    anything.

                         ANX
                    Really?

ALEX
Really. You are the most annoying thing in my life. Yet, I still need you… sometimes.

Anx makes a heart symbol by using her hands.

ALEX
But promise me that you'll focus on the positive for a while.

ANX
Fine. I'll do my best.

Alex checks the time and stands up immediately.

ALEX
Oh fuck! I should be on stage in an hour.

Alex sniffs her shirt, making a face.

ALEX (CONT'D)
Shit, I need to take a shower. I'll call the cab now.

ANX
I'll come with you.

Both exit.

WILDSMITH

(Excerpt of a TV comedy-drama)


Written by

Christopher Linforth










Christopher Linforth is a fiction writer and now writer for the stage and screen. His last book—The Distortions—received positive reviews in many outlets, including The Washington Post. He writes stories about interesting characters and unusual situations and worlds, including a poet and his translator in 1980s West Berlin, two old school friends in 1991 Zagreb arguing over the war, and a stage adaptation of Chekhov's "The Lady with the Dog" set in 2014 Crimea.

christopherlinforth@gmail.com

## EPISODE 1

FADE IN:

INT/EXT. WILDSMITH'S PRIVATE QUARTERS IN BARTON GRANGE — DAY

A grand room with a book-lined wall and a writing desk and leather sofa. By the fireplace, WILDSMITH (49), handsome, a little craggy, stands in the shadow of the large portrait of his father, WILDSMITH SNR (70s). On the mantelpiece sits poetry awards and volumes of poetry that all bear the name WILDSMITH. He turns away from the portrait. KEVIN (40), his assistant, stands by the door.

> WILDSMITH
> I don't know how long I can keep doing this.

Pause.

> KEVIN
> (nervously)
> One more summer?

There's some noise and commotion coming from the graveled drive at the front of the house. WILDSMITH goes to the window. He watches the parade of vehicles coming into the drive and parking up. A handful of strange-looking, artistic people exit their cars, making a fuss.

> WILDSMITH
> Yes, one more.

FADE OUT.

**WILDSMITH CREDIT SEQUENCE**

FADE IN:

INT/EXT. DARTMOOR COUNTRYSIDE — DAY

AMELIA (21) is driving her vintage Citroën 2CV down a country lane in remote Dartmoor. She's talking on her mobile with her boyfriend JACK (20). We hear a little of JACK's indistinct chatter.

                    AMELIA
          I don't know where I am. I'm lost.

Beat.

                    AMELIA (CONT'D)
          The GPS doesn't work.

Beat.

                    AMELIA (CONT'D)
          Jack, come on, that's not fair.

Beat.

                    AMELIA (CONT'D)
          I'm coming back.

Beat.

                    AMELIA (CONT'D)
          I am. I swear.

Beat.

                    AMELIA (CONT'D)
          I'll see you before I go to the US.

Beat.

                    AMELIA (CONT'D)
          Don't say that. I—

AMELIA's phone cuts out.

                    AMELIA (CONT'D)
          Hello Jack, are you still there?

AMELIA looks at her phone then throws it in the passenger seat. As she drives, she scouts for a sign for Barton Grange. AMELIA sees a woman (SINEAD, 40s, in her underwear and T-shirt) bent over in a boggy field. AMELIA pulls over and waves.

                    AMELIA
          Hi!

SINEAD ignores AMELIA. AMELIA exits her car and comes to a wooden gate. It's now clear that SINEAD is rubbing wet mud onto her bare legs.

                    AMELIA (CONT'D)
            Hello, excuse me, I'm looking for
            Barton Grange.

SINEAD beckons AMELIA to join her. AMELIA climbs over the
gate and joins SINEAD on the edge of a large muddy puddle.

                    SINEAD
                (Irish accent)
            I can only talk to other creatures
            of the bog.

Beat.

AMELIA hesitantly steps into the puddle.

                    SINEAD (CONT'D)
            Hold out your hand.

AMELIA complies and SINEAD draws a mud circle on AMELIA's
palm.

                    SINEAD (CONT'D)
            Now, we can speak.

                    AMELIA
            Barton Grange?

                    SINEAD
            Are you Amazon?

                    AMELIA
            No. I'm interning there this summer.

                    SINEAD
            Shame, I'm waiting on a parcel.

SINEAD takes off her shirt and rubs mud on her belly.

                    SINEAD (CONT'D)
            I wonder what happened to Andrea?

AMELIA looks away, a bit embarrassed.

                    SINEAD (CONT'D)
            Last year's intern. She fancied
            herself a writer, a poet. Funny
            girl, though. I didn't see her
            write anything. Maybe she was too
            intimidated by the old man.

                    AMELIA
          I'm inspired by his work. I love
          everything about his poetry.

SINEAD appears a little puzzled, almost bemused.

                    AMELIA (CONT'D)
          I'm Amelia.

                    SINEAD
          I'm a bog fairy.

Beat.

                    SINEAD (CONT'D)
          This is where I gather my strength.
          (points to the muddy puddle) I've
          been born and reborn here a thousand
          times.

AMELIA looks at the dark puddle.

                    AMELIA
          It's lovely.

                    SINEAD
          Barton Grange draws us to such
          places and new experiences. If
          you're ready for that, it's that
          gray dot on the horizon. (points)

They both look.


INT. AMELIA'S CAR — DAY — CONTINUOUS

AMELIA dashes off a poem title in her notebook: "The Bog Fairy."


EXT. LANE — DAY — CONTINUOUS

AMELIA drives off down the lane. We see SINEAD's underwear tossed up into the air.

INT/EXT. AMELIA'S CAR — DAY — CONTINUOUS

At long last AMELIA has a good view of Barton Grange in the near distance. She smiles at the beauty of the grand house.

INT. WILDSMITH'S PRIVATE QUARTERS — DAY

WILDSMITH sits at his writing desk attempting to compose a poem. On the desk is his notebook and a glass of whisky. KEVIN is arranging books on the bookshelf.

> WILDSMITH
> Who's that now?

KEVIN hurries to the window and sees Amelia's car pull up.

> KEVIN
> Looks like the new girl… The help.

Beat.

> KEVIN (CONT'D)
> She's a poet.

WILDSMITH makes a dismissive tutting sound.

> WILDSMITH
> I hope you chose *this one* wisely.

> KEVIN
> She has a poet's eye for detail, a poet's ear for lang—

> WILDSMITH
> I don't want her poet's mouth bothering me. Make sure she settles in downstairs.

KEVIN nods and heads to the door.

EXT. BARTON GRANGE DRIVE — DAY

AMELIA steps out of her car and looks around, a little dismayed at the state of the crumbling grand house. She stares up at the window where WILDSMITH is watching her. AMELIA waves. WILDSMITH closes the shutters.

INT. BARTON GRANGE FOYER — DAY — CONTINUOUS.

The foyer's plastered walls are full of cracks. The noticeboard has a couple of handmade posters: "Bankers are Wankers" and "My Other Poem's in the *New Yorker*." KEVIN runs up to AMELIA who is carrying her suitcase.

> AMELIA
> I'm sorry I'm late, my phone lost its signal.

AMELIA and KEVIN shake hands. KEVIN looks at his hand, sees the mud.

> KEVIN
> I see you met Sinead.

KEVIN takes a hankie from his pocket and wipes his hand.

> KEVIN (CONT'D)
> Anyway, I should have told you before. There's no signal around here for miles.

KEVIN leads AMELIA through the foyer.

> KEVIN (CONT'D)
> If you need to call someone, we have a payphone.

KEVIN points to the payphone. A woman (SARAH, 30s, American) is on the phone.

> SARAH (into the phone)
> I thought you had a deal with them… What do you mean they passed?

SARAH looks visibly upset.

> SARAH (CONT'D)
> How am I going to pay rent?

KEVIN slings her arm around AMELIA and directs her away from SARAH.

> KEVIN
> Let's go to your room.

INT. AMELIA'S BEDROOM — DAY — CONTINUOUS

The room is simple and clean. There's a bed and a wooden desk near the window.

KEVIN
I'll let you settle in.

AMELIA
Can I meet Wildsmith?

KEVIN
He's busy at the moment.

AMELIA
I'd just like to thank him.

KEVIN
Maybe after dinner. He's nicer then.

KEVIN leaves the room. AMELIA places her suitcase on the desk and removes a few poetry books. As she arranges them on the desk, a group of artists walk by her window. AMELIA goes to the window and sees the artists disappear into some ramshackle outbuildings. AMELIA returns to her desk and grabs a book that has WILDSMITH's name on the cover.

INT. BARTON GRANGE FOYER — DAY — CONTINUOUS

SARAH is slumped beneath the payphone. She holds the receiver to her neck.

AMELIA
(smiling)Do you know where I can find Wildsmith?

SARAH
Which one?

AMELIA
I don't un—

SARAH hears someone speak on the phone and so shushes AMELIA. AMELIA continues to stand there. SARAH, irritated, points upstairs.

INT. WILDSMITH'S QUARTERS — DAY — CONTINUOUS

The door sign notes "Private Quarters." AMELIA sees WILDSMITH through the ajar door. She knocks quietly. She waits for a second then walks in. WILDSMITH sits at his writing desk, his notebook blank. He holds a letter from the Arts Council saying funding won't be renewed for Barton Grange.

WILDSMITH
Go away.

AMELIA approaches WILDSMITH at his desk. WILDSMITH places the letter inside his notebook, closes it, closes his notebook and turns around.

WILDSMITH (CONT'D)
I'm working.

AMELIA
I thought I'd introduce myself…

WILDSMITH
Who are you?

AMELIA
Amelia…you chose me to come here…

WILDSMITH grunts.

AMELIA (CONT'D)
You've always been a hero of mine…
Your poetry moves me… I quote it all the time.

AMELIA appears just about to quote a line.

WILDSMITH
Please don't, not now.

AMELIA
Can you sign this?

AMELIA presents a book. WILDSMITH glances at it. He seems surprised.

AMELIA (CONT'D)
From one poet to another.

WILDSMITH takes the book, studies it for a moment, then flings it out of the door.

                    WILDSMITH
          Out.

AMELIA is upset. She hurries out into the hall and closes the door. She cries a little. KEVIN comes out of the room adjacent to WILDSMITH's quarters.

                    KEVIN
          I heard shouting. Is everything
          okay?

                    AMELIA
          I don't understand what I did wrong.

                    KEVIN
          I told you not to speak to him until
          after dinner.

                    AMELIA
          I just asked for his autograph.
          I love his poetry.

KEVIN picks up the book and studies the cover for a moment.

                    KEVIN
          This is his father's book.

KEVIN hands AMELIA the book. She makes a face as she realizes her mistake.

FADE OUT.

SPLINTER

(An extract from a play)

Written by

Martha Loader

Martha is a playwright, actor and producer from Ipswich. Previous work has been presented by HighTide, Mercury Theatre, Cambridge Junction, and INK. She is an associate artist of the New Wolsey Theatre and is currently working on commissions from Menagerie Theatre Company, and the Almeida Theatre. Her play Bindweed won the Judges Award at the Bruntwood Prize for Playwriting 2022 and will tour in 2024.

marthaloader@gmail.com / @marthaloader (Twitter)

**CHARACTERS**

Maggie – mid thirties
Jac 1 – mid thirties
Jac 2 – mid fifties
Peace Lily – a plant

**NOTES**

The play spans about 20 years.

No attempt should be made to 'age up' **Maggie**. She remains the age at which **Maggie** and **Jac** meet.

Props aren't necessary and can be alluded to through dialogue / sound effects.

( / ) indicates the next speech begins at that point.
Or, when at the end of a line, indicates the next speaker interrupting them.

(–) indicates a change of thought within the speech.

( , ) indicates a pause in dialogue.

\*

*Maggie stands, facing out.*

*She holds a ceramic blue plaque in her hands.*

*Turns it over.*

*Feeling the rough of the pottery on one side.*

*The smooth of the glaze on the other.*

*She turns it over and over in her hands.*

*Then she hangs it centre stage.*

*It looks a bit like the moon.*

*A high pitched sound starts up.*

*Maybe the lights dim or flicker.*

\*

Front garden

*Jac 1 enters.*

*She sees Maggie hanging the homemade blue plaque.*

          Jac 1

Oi.

Oi!

*Maggie stumbles slightly, caught off guard.*

          Maggie

Oops.

          Jac 1

The fuck are you doing?

          Maggie

Sorry!

          Jac 1

Are you, are you actually /serious?

          Maggie

/Sorry.

          Jac 1

I've just bought this place.

          Maggie

And I'm making it better. Adding value.

*She resumes her task.*

          Jac 1

That's, that's vandalism. You're vandalising my brand new shiny / house.

          Maggie

/Is it?

          Jac 1

No, it's ex-council but it cost me a fortune.

Maggie
Well now it's unique.

Jac 1
Can you stop. Please?
What is that? Plaster?

Maggie
Maybe.

Jac 1
Ah, that'll never come off.

Maggie
That's kind of the idea.

Jac 1
I should call the police.

Maggie
Ok. Well, ask for Derek. He's the one in charge of my case.

Jac 1
You're a renowned vandal?

Maggie
If you like.

Jac 1
For god's –
What are you doing? What are –
What is this?

Maggie
I knew you'd be interested.

Jac 1
I'm not interested. I'm just –
I'm giving you a chance to redeem yourself before I call Derek. The police.

Maggie
Well, I'm delighted you asked. This is Gladys Turnpike. She was part of a group of women who took part in a demonstration outside Parliament demanding the vote for women. She spent a week in prison for her

crimes and she lived here. So.
I'm recognising her. Properly.

> Jac 1

It's not exactly 'properly', is it? What's this? Did you make that yourself?

> Maggie

Yea.

> Jac 1

It's a bit shit.

> Maggie

I'm a revolutionary, not an artist.

> Jac 1

You're telling me.
How many of these have you done?

> Maggie

Plaques? About thirty.

> Jac 1

And no one minds?

> Maggie

Oh no, they mind. I mostly get the same reaction as yours. But once people hear the story, they tend to come around to the idea.

> Jac 1

And keep them on their walls?

> Maggie

Huh?

> Jac 1

You've gone back to check?

> Maggie

What?

> Jac 1

That they haven't instantly taken them down when you're gone.

                    Maggie
Well, no. But they always seem genuinely interested, so I /doubt they'd –

                    Jac 1
/There's no way.

                    Maggie
You're wrong. People are actually proud to be living in the same house as a /famous woman.

                    Jac 1
/Absolutely not the case. People don't care about women's history.

                    Maggie
They do once I've finished talking to them.

                    Jac 1
And how do you manage that?

                    Maggie
I build up a rapport. Talk to them about the significance.

                    Jac 1
Is that what you were doing just now?

                    Maggie
I

                    Jac 1
Because it really felt like you were just going to whack that up there and then leg it.

                    Maggie
Well people aren't always that/ keen.

                    Jac 1
Aha! Knew it.

                    Maggie
As you said, lots of people don't care about women's history. Including yourself.

                    Jac 1
I didn't say that.

                    Maggie
You implied it.

*Pause.*

*A stand-off.*

It is a lovely house.

                    Jac 1
Oh.

Thank you.

                    Maggie
Here by yourself?

                    Jac 1
Er, yea. I mean obviously I'm haemorrhaging money.

                    Maggie
I can imagine.

                    Jac 1
But it's worth it.

                    Maggie
Sure.

*Pause.*

Are you a Tory?

                    Jac 1
Excuse me?

                    Maggie
No, I just wondered. Because of /the -

                    Jac 1
/Because I can afford my own home?

                    Maggie
Yes...

> Jac 1
> It's really none of your /business.

> Maggie
> /So you are.

> Jac 1
> It doesn't make me a bad person.

> Maggie
> Sure, no.

> Jac 1
> You're saying that like it is.

> Maggie
> I'm not.

> Jac 1
> Yes you are. You're making it out that I'm some uptight, greedy, ISA owning… homeowner twat. While you're servant to the people, putting up your bloody, your bloody shitty homemade ode to dead people, taking over people's property like fucking… Stalin. Well, Stalin killed between ten and twenty, twenty million people and and raped and pillaged a load more.

'

So.

*Pause.*

> Maggie
> Well not single-handedly.

'

I have the same birthday as Stalin as it happens.
And Brad Pitt.

*Pause.*

I actually kinda fancy Tories.

> Jac 1
> Oh. Really? Ha, no you don't.

> Maggie
> Yea. I don't know what it is. Maybe the challenge.

> Jac 1
> That's, that seems /a bit —

> Maggie
> /So are you calling Derek, or can I finish putting up my plaque?

*Pause.*

> Jac 1
> She was a Suffragette?

> Maggie
> Yea.

> Jac 1
> And she definitely lived here?

> Maggie
> Yea.

*Pause.*

> Jac 1
> Ok then.

**Maggie** *smiles. Victorious.*

*Pause.*

> Do you, um
>
> Would you fancy a cuppa, um...

> Maggie
> Maggie.

> Jac 1
> Jac.
> Do you want a cuppa, Maggie?

\*

**Police Station**

*Jac 2 enters. Jac 1 exits.*

> Jac 2
> Do you want a cuppa?
> Maggie?
> I can get one from the machine?

> Maggie
> Sorry.

> Jac 2
> Don't
> It's fine.
> I don't like it when you say sorry.
> You don't need to say sorry.

> Maggie
> Sorry.

*Pause.*

> Jac 2
> Sounds like it'll just be a caution.

> Maggie
> Right.

> Jac 2
> So, you know
> It's fine.

> Maggie
> Why are they keeping us then?

> Jac 2
> To teach you a lesson probably.

*Jac 2 rubs her eyes.*

> Maggie
> Ok?

> Jac 2
> I took a tablet last night. I don't think it's quite out of my system yet.

>           Maggie
> You shouldn't have driven.
>
>           Jac 2
> Didn't have much choice.

*Maggie* squeezes *Jac 2's* hand.

*They soften.*

> Couldn't you sleep again?
>
>           Maggie
> No.
>
>           Jac 2
> I can't tell which of us is keeping the other awake.
>
>           Maggie
> You were flat out.
>
>           Jac 2
> Drugs'll do that.
> Maybe you should think about it.
>
>           Maggie
> Maybe.
>
>           Jac 2
> Might do you good –
>
>           Maggie
> Yea.
>
>           Jac 2
> Just to rest. Just get a full night in.
>
>           Maggie
> Yea maybe.
>
>           Jac 2
> What do you think about? Is it work?
>
>           Maggie
> Not really.
> I don't know. It's not really anything. You know how it is. Brain just goes –

Every now and then.

> **Jac 2**
> Yea, well it's just, it's been a while now. You must be running on empty.

*Pause.*

What made you think of it. Today? You haven't, not in –

> **Maggie**
> Of…

> **Jac 2**
> I'm just surprised, you know. I thought maybe it was all behind you. Who were you plaquing?

> **Maggie**
> Oh.
>
> Sarah Fosteque.

> **Jac 2**
> Suffragette?

> **Maggie**
> Rogue juror. Dressed up as her husband so she could attend court.

> **Jac 2**
> That's a good one.

> **Maggie**
> Yea well. The house owners didn't think so.

> **Jac 2**
> Huh.

*Pause.*

> **Maggie**
> Why do people take them down? The plaques.

> **Jac 2**
> They're not very good, darling.

>                    Maggie
> Prick.

*Jac 2 smiles.*

>                    Jac 2
> I never did.

>                    Maggie
> No.


\*

**Home.**

*Jac 2 pins blue disks up around the stage.*

*They look like blue plaques.*

*She talks through the disks as she pins.*

>                    Jac 2
> My number.
> Your sister's number.
> Frank and Jenny.
> Doctors, hairdresser, garage.
> Lockbox code.
> Simon.
> Pete.
> Nat and Dev.
> Oh and Elise but I'll, maybe I'll take that one down.
> Anything I've forgotten...

*Maggie enters.*

> Ok?

>                    Maggie
> Ok.

\*

**Festival**

*Jac 1 and **Maggie** are dancing.*

*Not well. Too self-conscious.*

*They catch each other's eyes. Laugh.*

          Jac 1
(shouts) I'm having a really great time!

          Maggie
(shouts) Me too!

          Jac 1
(shouts) I don't really know this band but they seem great.

          Maggie
(shouts) What?

          Jac 1
(shouts) The band!

*Jac 1 does a thumbs up.*

          Maggie
(shouts) Oh. Yea!

***Maggie** does a thumbs up.*

          Jac 1
(shouts) And it's not raining anymore. I think I can feel my skin again.

          Maggie
(shouts) Exactly!
I'm glad we came.

          Jac 1
What?

          Maggie
I'm glad we came. I really like being with you. I feel safe, somehow. I dunno. Do you know?

                    Jac 1
          *(unhearing)* Sure, yea.

                    Maggie
          I'm not saying that I -

          I don't think. I just, I don't know
          what it is. We just get on. Really
          easily. Weirdly easily. Because
          we shouldn't. You're... and I'm...
          but we do and I suppose I should
          just see that as a a a

          I didn't really think I'd meet
          someone. I've been pretty happy
          just, you know, just dicking around
          really. I'd kind of accepted that
          I probably wouldn't, and I'm not
          saying that you're

          And maybe you'll turn out to be
          a psychopath and kill me in my
          sleep or you'll have a gambling
          addiction and steal all the money
          in our account, or you'll turn out
          to be my long-lost half-sister and
          we'll have no choice but to kill
          ourselves. But at the moment you
          seem so much better than anyone else
          I've ever met so I'm willing to take
          the risk. Because I guess if you
          never take a risk, you never know.
          And it's better to have been with
          someone amazing who turns out to be
          somehow related to you than to have
          never tried at all, right?

                    Jac 1
          *(again unhearing)* Yup.
          Do you want to go away from the
          speakers? I think my eardrums have
          melted.

*She gestures to one side.*

**Maggie** *nods.*

*They move.*

          Sorry, I just, I couldn't really
          hear you properly. What were you
          saying?

> Maggie
> It doesn't matter.

> Jac 1
> Ok.

*Silence.*

> Maggie
> The band's really… really great.

> Jac 1
> Yea. Yea I love, er, this kind of music.

> Maggie
> Me too, yea.

*Pause.*

> Jac 1
> Although some of their songs went on for a really long time.

> Maggie
> Right?

> Jac 1
> And does it have to be *so loud?*

> Maggie
> You hate festivals, don't you?

> Jac 1
> What? No –

> Maggie
> Oh thank god, me too.

> Jac 1
> I only came because I thought you loved them.

> Maggie
> What?

> Jac 1
> Well, look at you. And Pete said –

                    Maggie
Pete? Pete's off his tits on legal
highs at these things and has no
idea what species he is by the end
of the weekend. He just assumes
everyone else is doing the same
thing.

                    Jac 1
Probably the only way to make it
bearable. There's just so much mud.

                    Maggie
And so many half-naked teenagers in
glitter.

                    Jac 1
We should probably find the others.

                    Maggie
Probably, yea.

                    Jac 1
They were talking about going to
that goat yoga workshop. That could
be fun.

                    Maggie
Yea.
Or

                    Jac 1
Go on.

                    Maggie
Or we ditch everyone, steal the car
and go home early?

                    Jac 1
Oh yea, that's a much better plan.
Forget what I said.

                    Maggie
Great.

*Pause.*

> Jac 1
> And I agree. Preferably I'd rather we weren't related, but I think you might be worth the risk too.

> Maggie
> You said you couldn't hear what I was saying!

> Jac 1
> I lied.

MUMMY'S WILL

(A short play)


Written by

Grace Maxted

Grace is a playwright and a poet. Her previous short plays have been performed in several theatres in and around London and internationally in Mumbai, India. Her most recent play was performed at Ink Festival 2024 and her poetry has been published in Popshot Magazine.

gracejmaxted@gmail.com

[LIGHTS UP]

[JENNY (48) bursts through the door to find HUGO (45) sitting on a step, his face propped up with his hands.]

JENNY: God, sorry, sorry, sorry! The trains were ludicrous — standing room only, and the standing area was filled with buggies, I swear there's some kind of baby epidemic sweeping south London. What'd I miss?

HUGO: It's gone.

JENNY: Where's the lawyer?

HUGO: Gone.

JENNY: I'm only fifteen minutes late.

HUGO: It was a short meeting.

JENNY: Hugo, what's happened?

HUGO: She's given it all to 'CATS'.

JENNY: You're joking — to a cat charity?

HUGO: No, literally 'CATS'. A revival of 'CATS: the musical'. She's donated it all to Andrew Lloyd Webber.

JENNY: Andrew Lloyd Webber, the billionaire?

HUGO: Yep.

JENNY: Oh. [BEAT] I'm sorry, what?

HUGO: Yeah.

JENNY: [She sits down next to HUGO] God, she really was batshit, wasn't she?

HUGO: *Catshit.*

JENNY: I mean, she did love that musical.

HUGO: Evidently more than us. Do you know how I spend my days, Jen? I get up at the arse crack of dawn, I have to put up with the relentless shit banter of the other lads, who are, by the way, all thick as two planks—

JENNY: Hugo–

HUGO: My hands are so dry they bleed! I go up and down stinkin' ladders all day, every day, and these days, if I so much as misplace my footing, my whole back goes. And she, she wants to give her money to a bunch of bleedin' actors poncing around dressed as human cats?! I can't, I just, I can't — I actually think I'm going to have a panic attack. Oh yes, here it comes.

JENNY: Ok, Hugo — breathe.

HUGO: [Hyperventilates] Ahhhh.

JENNY: Ok, one thing you can touch.

[HUGO grabs the banister]

Good, one thing you can see.

HUGO: [Looks up] Er…the door.

JENNY: One thing you can taste…

HUGO: [Continues to hyperventilate] Vomit. Ohhh, this isn't helping. Music helps.

[JENNY starts to hum 'Midnight...not a sound from the pavement…'

('Memory' from 'CATS').

HUGO eventually stops breathing heavily and looks at her.]

JENNY: Sorry, it's the only song I could think of. Ohhh, what are we going to do?

HUGO: There ain't much we can do. Those were her wishes.

JENNY: Can we plead insanity?

HUGO: She's already dead, Jen.

JENNY: Ok, well then - I don't know, 'duress', erm... 'improper pressure'–

HUGO: If you want to accuse Andrew Lloyd Webber of putting a gun to her head and asking her to change

|  |  |
|---|---|
|  | her will, be my guest. |
| JENNY: | Well, there must be a way around it. We're her children for Christ's sake. Who's the executor? |
| HUGO: | Who'd you think? |
| JENNY: | Jerry. |
| HUGO: | Fucking Jerry. |
| JENNY: | So, this is his doing. |
| HUGO: | I don't think that's a thing. |
| JENNY: | Has he not got a penny of it either? |
| HUGO: | I don't think so - I found him weeping at the bottom of the steps here when he got the envelope. |
| JENNY: | [Claps her hands in triumph] Ha! All those years sucking up to an old grandma, to no avail. |
| HUGO: | He did help her do things around the house. Saved me a few jobs over the years. |
| JENNY: | I never trusted him, he's so creepy. He stares at me. [BEAT] And I'll never forgive him for making us feel terrible that she'd had to spend Christmas Day with him. I'd invited her! She didn't want to come, said she'd rather be on her own. |
| HUGO: | We invited her n' all. |
| JENNY: | There's got to be another way - I had my thighs done on the proviso I was due some money. Can't exactly get a refund. |
| HUGO: | I just got myself a new shed. Well, it's called a Shepherd's Hut - one of those fancy ones you can sleep in. |
| JENNY: | That because your wife hates you? She'd have probably paid for that out of her own money, |

155.

|        |                                                                                                                                                                                                                                                                 |
|--------|-----------------------------------------------------------------------------------------------------------------------------------------------------------------------------------------------------------------------------------------------------------------|
|        | gladly.                                                                                                                                                                                                                                                         |
| HUGO:  | About the only thing she would.                                                                                                                                                                                                                                 |
| JENNY: | Wait a second, Mummy always said: 'If anything ever happens to me, everything is in the turquoise notebook.' Maybe she's left further instructions that might supersede the will?                                                                               |
| HUGO:  | Nah, I've already looked in it - it's just notes for Andrew, some suggestions for changes to the revival and drawings of cats.                                                                                                                                  |
| JENNY: | Jesus Christ!                                                                                                                                                                                                                                                   |
| HUGO:  | Superstar. I got a suit for this.                                                                                                                                                                                                                               |
| JENNY: | So I can see, Marks and Spencer - a classic.                                                                                                                                                                                                                    |
| HUGO:  | Ohh, don't be such a snob!                                                                                                                                                                                                                                      |
| JENNY: | I'm not!                                                                                                                                                                                                                                                        |
| HUGO:  | You are. You changed your accent soon as you hit puberty.                                                                                                                                                                                                       |
| JENNY: | No, I just started speaking like an adult. You changed your accent - you became more 'wide boy', more 'Laandon', just so you could fit in with the other apprentices.                                                                                           |
| HUGO:  | But my name is fucking Hugo. Do you know how much they rip the shit out of me for that? They go: 'Oh Hugo - la di dar!' about everything! 'Sushi for lunch? La di dar!' 'A Shepherd's Hut? La di dar!' I've stopped telling 'em my weekend plans…but it'd be far worse if I didn't speak like this. |
| JENNY: | Yes, but I don't think I've ever heard you say the word 'isn't' - it's ain't this, ain't that. And by the way, there's a 't' in the middle of the word 'water'. [BEAT] The suit's nice, it suits you. |

HUGO: It's alright for you, you married money. Not worked a day in your life! Never saw him working for it neither.

JENNY: I married a man with money, who then had to give me a large portion of that money, when he started spending that money on having sex with other women. I'll have you know that I've worked. Marriage is work, Hugo.

HUGO: Yeah, yeah.

JENNY: I knew exactly how that marriage was going to play out-

HUGO: Did you fuck.

JENNY: And I worked for that settlement. [BEAT] Maybe I'm just more emotionally intelligent than you are, Hugo.

HUGO: Oh, it was in the bin, was it?

JENNY: It's 'in the bag', darling.

HUGO: Sorry, not all of us went to finishing school.

JENNY: You didn't go to any bloody school, you bunked off about 60% of secondary school.

HUGO: To spend more time with my dear, old mother! [He laughs then begins to sob].

JENNY: Are you crying about Mummy or about the money?

HUGO: Both.

JENNY: Save it for the eulogy. Hugo, what are we actually going to do?!

HUGO: Why are you even bothered about the money? You're sorted.

JENNY: I'm not. Barry's settlement wasn't quite enough. Honestly Hugo, I'm struggling to afford the rent at the moment. I'm in Cardboard bloody City.

HUGO: You could go and live with Jerry, I'm sure he'd have you.

[JENNY shudders]

JENNY: Well, with any luck, Jerry will throw himself down the stairs in despair and we'll have made it into his will somewhere.

HUGO: Hmm...so long as he hasn't left it to Lin-Manual Miranda.

JENNY: More likely 'Magic Mike Live!', I reckon.

[They both laugh]

Hang on, how do you know Lin-Manual Miranda?

HUGO: TikTok innit? 17...se se 17, 1789.

JENNY: Oooh, la di dar!

[Their laughter fades]

Do you remember when we used to put the chip ends she burnt under the sofa?

HUGO: Yep, she'd go mental when she found them about six months later.

JENNY: She did. She walloped you for that once, didn't she?

HUGO: Yep, I took one for the team. It wasn't terrible. Probably why I'm into such weird, kinky stuff these days.

JENNY: Ewwww! Come on.

HUGO: What? It's true - Freud was all over it.

JENNY: Do you remember when we used to dance to MJ in the dining room?

HUGO: Yeah.

[Silence]

JENNY: She never liked any of my boyfriends.

HUGO: She did.

| | |
|---|---|
| JENNY: | Nope, I know she didn't like Barry. She liked his money though, oh yes, another all-inclusive cruise paid for? Don't mind if I do! |
| | [HUGO chuckles] |
| | You know, I don't think she ever actually liked me. |
| HUGO: | Nah, she was jealous of you. |
| JENNY: | What? No she wasn't. |
| HUGO: | She was – you were effortlessly stunning and she had even features, but wasn't exactly a show-stopper was she? |
| JENNY: | Aw, thanks little bro. |
| HUGO: | I did say 'were'. |
| JENNY: | Hey! [She punches him in the arm] |
| HUGO: | No, you are. You know you're beautiful. Barry's an idiot. |
| JENNY: | Barry is an idiot. |
| HUGO: | Especially with your new thighs. |
| JENNY: | Why are you being so weird and inappropriate? |
| HUGO: | Grief – it does mysterious things. Plus this [he pulls out a hip flask and takes a swig from it], this was hers. I'm not gonna be able to drive you home. |
| JENNY: | You come in the van? |
| HUGO: | Yeah. |
| JENNY: | In your new suit? |
| HUGO: | I put a sheet down. |
| | [JENNY nods and ponders] |
| JENNY: | You know, she'd always say to me: 'Stop frowning, stop frowning'. So I got…well, Barry paid for me to have Botox and then she said: 'Why've you gone and done that for? Destroyed that beautiful |

|   |   |
|---|---|
|   | face!'. Well, now we haven't got this money and Barry's payments are drying up, parts of me will start dropping off and caving in. I'll be like the bloody Scarecrow in the 'Wizard of Oz'! This is a lot of maintenance, you know? Costs a bloody fortune… |
| HUGO: | My therapist said that she sabotaged us - you know, like, undermined us, or whatever. |
| JENNY: | Your therapist? |
| HUGO: | Yes, you're not the only one in the world with problems, you know. |
| JENNY: | Aw, you getting bullied again? |
| HUGO: | Fuck off [voice cracks]. I'm just so up and down, Jen. |
|   | [JENNY reaches out to hold his hand] |
| JENNY: | Oh, love. |
| HUGO: | I mean, what did the bloody woman want? |
| JENNY: | A revival of 'CATS' apparently. [BEAT] No, I think she wanted us to be closer, you know, growing up. |
| HUGO: | How much closer? We were-. Are. |
| JENNY: | I mean, you don't call a lot. |
| HUGO: | Neither do you. |
| JENNY: | Well, I've had enough on my pla- [looks at him] l mean, maybe we should rectify that. |
| HUGO: | Do you think we ever actually made her proud? |
| JENNY: | Well, I did. I'm joking, that's a joke. |
| HUGO: | Ha ha. |
| JENNY: | I'm sure we did…on some level. And without sounding harsh, it kind of doesn't really matter |

|        | now, does it? Anyway, remember, 'we are all works in progress'. |
|--------|---|
| HUGO:  | See that on a coaster, did you? |
| JENNY: | No, it's what I have to tell myself when a procedure doesn't quite do the trick. |
|        | [JENNY takes the hip flask and drinks] |
|        | Wow, I think I'm actually going to miss her. |
| HUGO:  | Like fuck I will. She was mean! |
| JENNY: | She was pretty mean. |
| HUGO:  | Mean-spirited. |
| JENNY: | Hmmm. [BEAT] Do you want to come home with me? |
| HUGO:  | I dunno. |
| JENNY: | We could get a takeaway. Do you want to watch the recording of 'CATS' on the fire stick? |
| HUGO:  | No, I bloody don't. |
| JENNY: | I have gin? Come on. |
|        | [JENNY helps HUGO up and puts her arm around him. They begin to exit.] |
|        | Well, I hope Lord Andrew is bloody grateful. Ooh, maybe we'll get to go to the premiere? |
| HUGO:  | I'd rather give myself a colonoscopy. |
| JENNY: | Oh god, there's an image. This the kinky shit you were referring to? |
|        | [LIGHTS DOWN] |

"I'LL BE A BOGGART TO YOU"

(A short film)


Written by

Mae Milburn

Mae is a playwright from Leeds. In 2016 they were shortlisted for the National Theatre's New Views playwriting competition. In 2024 they were the recipient of the Snoo Wilson Prize for their play Dirty Angel. Their work has been produced by Slung Low.

mae.rose.milburn@gmail.com

EXT. MYTHOLMROYD MOOR, DAY 1

Wind shakes the heather. A rocky path. A stream. A bog. A cairn. The land is humming. Singing.

EXT. COUNTRYSIDE, DAY 1

ANNA, 24, walks a country lane, camping gear strapped to her back. It's spring and the land is coming back to life. She sees Stoodley Pike in the distance.

EXT. STOODLEY PIKE, DAY 1

The Stoodley Pike Monument looms over ANNA, an enormous stone obelisk. She has the place to herself. She inspects the doorway. Inside is a spiral staircase that trails off into complete darkness. She dumps her bag and starts to climb it.

EXT. MONUMENT BALCONY, DAY 1

Wind blows her hair madly. She leans over the balcony. The entire Calderdale Valley is at her feet, it's beautiful. She shouts. The wind snatches her voice away. This pleases her. She pauses. She screams, guttural, angry.

EXT. COUNTRYSIDE, DAY 1

On the path away from the pike, ANNA is loaded with camping gear again.

Her phone starts to buzz over and over. She's just got signal. There are 3 missed calls from "Mum" and a string of texts, *'Just let me know how you're getting on...'*, *'Please let me know...'*, *'I can't stop you from doing what you want...'*.

ANNA doesn't read them, she types out *'Not Dead'* and sends it. She pauses. Then takes a picture of the view and sends that too.

EXT. COUNTRYSIDE, DAY 1

ANNA crosses through the wind-swept heather. It's getting darker now.

She climbs the rocky path.

Walks through the stream.

Arrives at the bog.

She steps carefully between stones and notices the cairn. She crouches to inspect it. A perfectly round, flat stone rests at the top of the pile. Anna picks this up and feels the weight of it in her palm.

CUT TO:

INT. HOSPITAL, MEMORY

We catch a glimpse of MARIE, 60, ANNA'S mother, under clinical sterile lighting. Her face is drained. Silent.

BACK TO:

EXT. BOG, EARLY EVENING

ANNA puts the stone in her pocket. She walks on.

By the cairn is a hare. There's something unnatural about its stillness, the way it's staring.

EXT. COUNTRYSIDE, EVENING

The light is fading. ANNA needs to find somewhere to camp. In the distance is a homestead. ANNA notices the figure of a MAN, far off behind her, walking the same path. She picks up her pace.

EXT. HOMESTEAD, NIGHT 1

An honesty box reads "HONESTY BOX, camping £5. *Do NOT feed Fudge the horse, he's on a diet*". ANNA puts her coins in.

Her tent is up. She cooks on a little camping stove.

She watches the night sky.

She climbs into her tent and zips it up.


EXT. HOMESTEAD, DAY 2

ANNA is asleep. The top half of her has been dragged out of her tent. She wakes up and realises where she is. She looks with suspicion at the farmhouse.

ANNA packs up her things quickly.


EXT. COUNTRYSIDE, DAY 2

ANNA walks through a field of cows. At the far side of a field a weathered old FARMER watches her. He's still. She waves at him. He doesn't wave back.


EXT. WOODS, DAY 2

A stretch of woodland. ANNA walks slowly, enjoying it. The leaves are coming back. She watches the light shining through them. The trickle of a river can be heard. She follows the sound.


EXT. RIVER BANK, WOODS, DAY 2

ANNA sits and takes her shoes and socks off. She puts her feet in the cold river, we hear the sound of her feet against pebbles. She runs her hands through the water. It's lovely.

The sound of pebbles moving startles her. She looks up to see a YOUNG MAN, 19, not too far upstream watching her. She gives him a weak smile. He's unresponsive. She starts drying her feet. The YOUNG MAN starts moving towards her. ANNA rushes to put her shoes and socks on. Grabs her bag and leaves.

EXT. FARMYARD, DAY 2

ANNA is on her phone, looking at the map. A LITTLE BOY, 5, is leaning against a gate post, swinging from side to side, watching her, blankly. ANNA smiles at him. She walks on, still looking at her phone.

The LITTLE BOY starts making a strange deep gurgling sound. He takes a step towards ANNA. She steps back.

The LITTLE BOY reaches into his mouth and from deep in his throat produces a hospital wristband. ANNA is horrified. She walks quickly, almost running. The LITTLE BOY stands in the road watching.


INT. MARIE'S HOUSE, EVENING, MEMORY

MARIE hesitates outside ANNA's ROOM.

The door is open, the room is in darkness. We can just about make out the shape of ANNA hunched over in bed.

MARIE takes a step forward but ANNA leaps off the bed and smashes the door shut. ANNA stands with her back to the door. She smashes the back of her head against it, over and over.

MARIE's face is inches from the wood of the door as ANNA BANG BANG BANGS against it.


INT. HOSPITAL, MEMORY

ANNA in a hospital bed. She won't look at MARIE. MARIE tries to take ANNA's limp hand. ANNA moves it away.


EXT. COUNTRYSIDE, EVENING, DAY 2

ANNA's tent is set up in a wild looking field. She turns the flat pebble over and over in her hand, staring at nothing.

INT./EXT. ANNA'S TENT, NIGHT 2

ANNA can't sleep. It's like she's waiting for something.

We hear the sound of something moving towards her in the long grass. There's a gurgling sound. ANNA lies there gathering the courage to face it.

She bolts upright and unzips the tent. She's face to face with BOGGART ANNA, an exact replica of herself. On hands and knees. Staring. Impassive.

ANNA breathes quickly, studying it back. She's angry. She slaps BOGGART ANNA across the face, hard. It doesn't react. She slaps it again, harder. And again. And again.

ANNA relents. She studies the BOGGART with sympathy.

She rummages amongst her things and produces the flat pebble. She holds it out for the BOGGART.

BOGGART ANNA takes the stone then grabs ANNA's wrist tightly, pulling her toward it. With its eyes it searches her, gives her a warning.

The BOGGART drops ANNA's wrist and turns to leave with its stone. ANNA watches it walk away through the field.


INT. MARIE'S HOUSE, EVENING, MEMORY

ANNA rests her head on MARIE's chest while watching TV.

MARIE strokes her hair.


INT. TRAIN, DAY 3

A little girl, sat with her mum, watches ANNA.

ANNA rests her head on the window. She opens her phone. Her thumb hovers over "Mum" in contacts.

The little girl is still staring at ANNA, blank, very still.


END.

SIGNAL FAILURE

(A stage play)


Written by

Jonathon Sims










Jonathon Sims is a writer based in Cambridge. He trained as an actor at Mountview Academy of Theatre Arts and has worked extensively in theatre and television. A lover of all forms of scriptwriting Jonathon's work spans everything from closely observed domestic comedy to wide ranging geo-political drama.

Jonathonsims00@gmail.com

## ACT [1] SCENE [1]

*A rumble of trains.*

*Lights come up on a railway station platform.*

*The station clock reads 07.22am.*

*A National Rail logo hangs with the station name, "Luton".*

*Stage left a"Way Out" sign hangs above the exit. Stage right sits an electrical cabinet with a "Danger of death" warning sign on the door.*

*Against the back wall are two benches left and right of centre. Between them is a triptych of posters:*

*An NHS ad."If you knew about flu you'd get the jab".*
*A "Counter Culture" music festival ad.*

*A New Scientist magazine ad. "The asteroid that's out to get you".*

*A "CCTV in operation" sign sits on the back wall near the exit. Below it a fire extinguisher, and a sand bucket.*

*A yellow "stand behind" line runs across the front of the stage.*

*A grey rucksack sits unattended in the middle of the yellow line.*

The STUDENT sits on the floor leaning against the electrical cupboard. He studies a textbook. He closes his eyes occasionally, mouthing words, then reads on.

The CONSULTANT sits on the stage right bench marking a report. He huffs and sighs, darting back and forth, scribbling furiously.

The SOCIAL WORKER sits on the left bench next to several bottles of protein shakes. She is labelling the shakes with a marker pen.

The LAWYER enters carrying some sheet music listening to an iPod. She sits next to The SOCIAL WORKER and plays music in her head.

*A few moments pass.*

The ARTIST enters wearing Audrey Hepburn sunglasses and big hat, closely followed by The HAIRDRESSER carrying a magazine. They take a position left and right of centre stage. The ARTIST touches up her appearance, The HAIRDRESSER flicks through his magazine. They exchange a look. A smile.

*Audio clip plays from London's successful bid to host the 2012 Olympics as-*

The ATHLETE enters from the stairwell. He jogs up and down, stretching his hamstrings. He goes to the rucksack and takes out a pair of boxing gloves and puts them on. He shadow boxes as he speaks.

THE ATHLETE    They called him the greatest. The man who could not be knocked down, put down, kept down. Yet even he had to lose. Had to lose that which he was not, before he could claim that which he was. You know what I'm sayin? Tch, no. No no. How could you know, how could anybody know. Only *you* know, you know *(he laughs)*. You think you're going to grow up great. Maybe not the greatest, but great you know. You got it all. I would not use the word superior, but you know. Strong, beautiful, advantaged in all kinds of ways. Tch, that's a lie. It's a lie we tell ourselves and a lie told to us by all men. Black, white no matter. Two sides of the same lie. One to lift you up, one to put you down. I don't believe no- one no more. Listening to all that stuff. You gotta fight against this, keep your eyes on him, don't get close to her. Remember she not like us. Like us, like who, like me? Like who are you to give me that point of view. Telling me who I am. Calling me names and you don't even know your own. So let's start there. With a name. With that by which we are known.

>                         It's time to go back to the land
>                         where we all learnt how to stand
>                         on nobody else's feet. Start
>                         with my name.

THE ARTIST takes the gloves off the ATHLETE and puts them back in the rucksack. From inside it she takes out a packet of cigarettes and hands one to The HAIRDRESSER who lights it.

THE ARTIST          How long does it take to smoke a cigarette?

THE HAIRDRESSER     I dunno. I've never timed myself.

THE ARTIST          Seriously. How long?

THE HAIRDRESSER     Seriously? OK. Well we have fifteen minute breaks at work. I reckon that's three to make the coffee. Quick slash. Check me hair. That takes time. I'm a hairdresser you see.

THE ARTIST          I can tell.

THE HAIRDRESSER     Easy five minutes I'd say. Then I have a fag with what's left. Hm, probably seven or eight minutes. Why?

THE ARTIST          Just wondering how many tube trains you have missed.

THE HAIRDRESSER     Having a fag? Oh hundreds.

THE ARTIST          In eight minutes?

THE HAIRDRESSER     I see. Three, maybe four. Depends on the line. She never goes out of fashion does she?

THE ARTIST          Who?

THE HAIRDRESSER     *(gestures her look)*
                    Holly Golightly.

THE ARTIST          Her look or her profession?

The ARTIST takes off her hat and flounces her hair.

THE ARTIST        Actually it *was* a present from a much older man. My father.

THE HAIRDRESSER   You not having one?

THE ARTIST        I don't. Not anymore. No more hanging about tube entrances for me.

THE HAIRDRESSER   You don't know what you're missing.

*There is a rumble of a train approaching. They ready themselves to board.*

The ARTIST puts her hat in the rucksack.

THE ARTIST        No time.

                                                    BLACKOUT.


## ACT [1] SCENE [2]


*Audio clip plays from a radio news programme about the Healthcare Commission taking over from the Commission for Healthcare Improvement.*

*Lights up on the same.*

The CONSULTANT takes out a folder from the rucksack and puts his report in it. He carries it under his arm and paces up and down.

THE CONSULTANT    This is not great, not great at all.

He considers all the other passengers and plumps for The LAWYER. Pulls the headphones out of her ears and brings her to the front of the stage.

THE CONSULTANT    I work for the government. Department of Health actually. Do you mind answering a few questions?

THE LAWYER        Well—

THE CONSULTANT  Unless you work for the Healthcare Commission of course in which case your answers would be invalid.

THE LAWYER  No. Accountant. Private equity.

THE CONSULTANT  Can we talk about your grandmother?

THE LAWYER  Sorry?

THE CONSULTANT  I'm gathering data.

THE LAWYER  Oh I see. Sure, it's just-

THE CONSULTANT  What?

THE LAWYER  My grandmother is no longer with us.

THE CONSULTANT  Perfect. I mean/you know. Hypothetical grandmothers are always better /in these situations.

THE LAWYER  Are they?

THE CONSULTANT  Much. So imagine your grandmother needs to go into hospital. First thing that happens is they have to put her into the system right?

THE LAWYER  Right.

THE CONSULTANT  And the problem with that is-

THE LAWYER  Well, um-

THE CONSULTANT  Your grandmother can get lost.

THE LAWYER  Pardon?

THE CONSULTANT  She gets registered as a patient then booked for an assessment right?

THE LAWYER  Right.

THE CONSULTANT  But if it turns out she needs to see a specialist in another hospital the process has to be done all over again.

THE LAWYER  Yes but at least she gets the right help.

THE CONSULTANT   True. But you see on discharge she gets put on a care plan from the same hospital.

THE LAWYER   What's wrong with that?

THE CONSULTANT   Because before anyone comes out to assess her she has a fall.

THE LAWYER   Poor old grandma.

THE CONSULTANT   She goes into the *original* hospital for treatment and goes back home. But social services have no idea they are now dealing with someone with a fractured hip.

THE LAWYER   How come?

THE CONSULTANT   Because no-one in their PCT knows about it. See the system is designed to follow her treatment, not her. It is as broken as the fragile bones in her body. No offence.

THE LAWYER   She's dead, none taken.

THE CONSULTANT   That's what I am trying to fix. Do you think you will? Given time.

*The rumble of an approaching train. The CONSULTANT puts the folder back in the rucksack and readies himself for boarding.*

BLACKOUT.

A CONVENIENT ADULT

(An extract from a play)

Written by

Nina Sumerling

Nina is a writer, musician and composer from Bury St Edmunds. She achieved a bachelor's in Theatre: Writing, Directing and Performance (University of York) before specialising in writing at the UEA. She has since received a short-film commission from the Sainsbury Centre, been nominated for a Young Norwich Creative Award and is undertaking multiple projects from socio-political drama to musical theatre and comedy.

ninasumerling@gmail.com

*Evie Bullen, 15, sits curled up atop a classroom table, the only one left standing. Around her is the wreckage of her recent outburst — knocked-over chairs, tables thrown on their sides and the contents of rucksacks strewn across the floor. There is also a cartoon of a fat pig wearing a top hat, sitting on a pile of cash, drawn on the whiteboard with indistinguishable writing below. Around the pig are GCSE standard maths equations which are rubbed out carelessly to accommodate the animal. Evie's hands are covered in ink.*

*Nancy Adams, the headteacher opens the door with cautious authority and seeing Evie is stable, strides over and stands before her.*

Nancy: Evie, it's Mrs Adams.

*No response.*

I came for a chat.

*Evie doesn't stir.*

You've made quite the mess.

*Nancy picks up a stranded chair, places it by Evie's table and sits, looking up at her.*

Lift your head.

*Evie twists her head to look in Nancy's direction but does not raise it.*

Did I mention it was Mrs Adams?

*Evie lifts her head and comes out of her ball, avoiding Nancy's gaze.*

Do you want to tell me what happened, or shall I take Mr Evan's word for it?

*Nothing. Nancy moves for the door.*

Then tidy up. I'll ring your

>           parents and we can discuss whether
>           you have a future here.
>
>           *Evie jumps to her feet.*

Evie:      Miss, don't.

Nancy:     Don't what?

Evie:      Expel me?

>           *Nancy considers this.*

Nancy:     Did you draw the pig?

Evie:      yeah.

Nancy:     It's good, I'll give you that.
           Shall we start by rubbing it
           out?

>           *Evie goes to the board and rubs
>           out the writing below quickly
>           with her hand.*

           Stop.

>           *Nancy goes to the teacher's desk
>           and pulls out an eraser, handing
>           it to Evie.*

Evie:      It's a he. Not an it.

Nancy:     Pardon?

Evie:      It's *Babe*. It's my favourite
           film. Made me a veggie.

>           *This stumps Nancy. She takes the
>           eraser back before Evie wipes
>           the board.*

Nancy:     I was surprised to hear about
           your behaviour this afternoon.
           You've always struck as more…
           perhaps rather more aware than
           many of your peers. Someone who
           uses her words. (*Beat*) Anyway,
           I have politics in here — twenty-
           minutes — so let's sort this.

Evie:      You teach?

Nancy:     It's in my title.

Evie:      Yeah, but I thought that the
           teacher part of headteacher
           was, well…you know how they call
           the prime minister's friends

|         |                                                                                                                                                                                                 |
|---------|-------------------------------------------------------------------------------------------------------------------------------------------------------------------------------------------------|
|         | government secretaries even though they've probably never done a days' typing in their lives.                                                                                                   |
| Nancy:  | Ben is sitting in my office with a bloody nose.                                                                                                                                                 |
| Evie:   | Well, he shouldn't…                                                                                                                                                                             |
| Nancy:  | Shouldn't…?                                                                                                                                                                                     |
| Evie:   | I'll tidy up for your politics, don't worry.                                                                                                                                                    |
| Nancy:  | I'm not worried.                                                                                                                                                                                |
|         | *Evie starts picking up the rucksack debris on the floor.*                                                                                                                                      |
|         | Was it politics that got you here by any chance? Mr Evans said it was another 'communist rant'.                                                                                                 |
| Evie:   | I didn't rant. Ben provoked *me,* not the other way round. He's been taking the piss out of me for months. I'd had it. And he thinks Lenin was in the Beatles for god's sake. If Evans -        |
| Nancy:  | *Mr* Evans said you punched Ben.                                                                                                                                                                |
| Evie:   | I *pushed* him. *He* pushed me.                                                                                                                                                                 |
| Nancy:  | Yet he's the one with a broken nose.                                                                                                                                                            |
| Evie:   | Broken?                                                                                                                                                                                         |
| Nancy:  | Quite probably.                                                                                                                                                                                 |
| Evie:   | Is he…? Shit. Sorry -                                                                                                                                                                           |
| Nancy:  | You're sorry?                                                                                                                                                                                   |
| Evie:   | I did say shit and I was gonna say fuck.                                                                                                                                                        |
| Nancy:  | So, you're not sorry for Ben?                                                                                                                                                                   |
| Evie:   | I'm sorry it's broken but I just reacted. Defended myself.                                                                                                                                      |
| Nancy:  | Not sorry you acted out?                                                                                                                                                                        |
|         | *Evie is confused.*                                                                                                                                                                             |
|         | You *are* sorry his nose may be broken, but not sorry you may have broken it.                                                                                                                   |

**Evie:** …sorry?

**Nancy:** You say you were retaliating, he provoked you, and he in turn retaliated against you. Therefore, you believe his broken nose is his fault not yours.

**Evie:** You gonna read my Miranda rights, miss?

**Nancy:** I'm just trying to work out what punishment is most suited to your behaviour and well, if you're not sorry…his nose is not broken, Evie, okay? It just appears –

**Evie:** So you lied? Why did you —

**Nancy:** (*voice raised*) Because it could have been! You could've done some real damage.

*This shuts Evie up.*

(*Calmer*) Don't you get bored of getting into trouble?

**Evie:** Talking about expelling me. That's quite interesting.

**Nancy:** Interesting how?

**Evie:** Seems a bit extreme. And I *am* sorry I hurt him.

**Nancy:** You're in my office most weeks. It always comes down to some political statement you've upset other students with and it needs to stop. You hurt Ben whether you meant to or not. You're practically an adult. You have to take responsibility.

**Evie:** I'm only an adult when it's convenient to the actual adults, otherwise I'm a stupid kid who knows nothing.

**Nancy:** Meaning?

**Evie:** Like, I've done something bad — even though I didn't mean to — and my whole future's threatened, my education,

|         | because 'I should know better 'cause I'm old enough'. But when I try to be responsible or at least I try to be interested in *political* responsibility — interest in the adult world I allegedly have a stake in, I'm laughed out 'cause I'm just a kid. I'm just a kid when I try, but when I fail, I'm an adult. I get it, I should be punished, but if I have to take *that* responsibility why can't I take responsibility for my own beliefs too? Evans just calls me naïve, but am I? Aren't I just new to things? How can you be naïve when you haven't had the chance to learn cause no one seriously talks to you about politics 'til you're a real adult? Yes, I get carried away. Yes, maybe I shouldn't go on as much as I do. But isn't it better to have an opinion now and share it so we can all learn what's out there to believe, even just as a starting point. Then I can be responsible when I can actually vote. I don't deserve to be bullied or censored for that, by Ben, Evans or anyone. |
|---|---|
| Nancy: | It's a fair argument. |
| Evie: | Is it? |
| Nancy: | No, I get it. Let's talk about this like grown-ups. |
|  | *Nancy rights a table from the floor and pulls it to one side. She moves Evie's upright table to the same side.* |
|  | Go on. |
|  | *Evie, confused, rights another table. Nancy points to the opposite side and Evie puts the table there. During the next line, they place other tables and chairs on either side so a* |

*gap is cleared down the middle.*

This is what I do with my sixth formers. We push the tables apart, I put them into groups, and I pose a statement. 'Nuclear weapons should be banned', 'The monarchy should be abolished'. One side argues the affirmative, the other the negative.

*The stage is set for debate. Nancy sits on one side.*

Sit, sit.

*Evie goes to sit next to Nancy.*

No. Over there. Come on.

*Evie goes to sit on the other side.*

You start. Tell me in the affirmative why 'Evie Bullen was justified in pushing Ben'.

Evie: He called me things. I felt threatened.

Nancy: Gonna need more than that. Evidence. What did he *do* that made you feel threatened?

Evie: Said things. 'Commie, Stalin', whatever. Stupid things he always says. And Evans only hears me telling Ben to watch his mouth. He tells me to mind myself, so I tell him what Ben was saying and I get this little lecture — the same one he always does — says I gotta stop being so sensitive, that I got a lot of growing up to do because 'communism doesn't work. Never has. Never will.' Not exactly being impartial I might add. Then he left, and Ben gets really close to me and calls me a 'backwards fascist', says 'your lot are always extremists'. He got so close.

Nancy: So, you punched him.

| | |
|---|---|
| Evie: | *Pushed* him – pushed! And he hurt me too – look at my arm. |
| | *Evie shows the scratches on her arm.* |
| | I'd call that evidence. |
| Nancy: | I'll take it into account. |
| Evie: | And I got so angry when Evans cleared everyone out of the class like I was some kind of animal. So, I trashed the room… proving his point somewhat. |
| Nancy: | And you drew an animal too? |
| Evie: | It's not *Babe,* it's a capitalist pig. |
| Nancy: | I guessed. I saw Mr Evans' name underneath. |
| Evie: | Sorry. |
| Nancy: | Can you sum up? |
| Evie: | Ben insulted me, it wasn't the first time. My beliefs and…well— |
| Nancy: | More concise. |
| Evie: | I only pushed him; I didn't mean to hurt him. Just to send him a message, get him away. He hit back. That's when I pushed him hard, and he hurt his nose. And to be honest, I was so pissed off at Evans – *Mr* Evans - and the class were all – |
| Nancy: | No new information. Quickly, list your main points. |
| Evie: | He insulted me, he got way too close, I was angry at Mr Evans, and I really didn't have any intention of hurting him. I was standing up for myself. I felt justified in getting him to back off and it seemed the only way. |
| | *Nancy claps.* |
| Nancy: | Not bad. Now come sit over here. |
| | *Evie and Nancy swap places.* |

|        | Now, tell me why 'you were wrong'. |
|--------|---|
| Evie:  | Can I abstain? |
| Nancy: | No. |
| Evie:  | I shouldn't have let myself get in such a state. I should have controlled myself. I didn't mean to hurt him, but I didn't feel bad about hurting him afterwards. That's wrong. I should have been the bigger person. And I should have apologised straight away instead of destroying your classroom. |
| Nancy: | Anything else? |
| Evie:  | Best I can do. |
| Nancy: | Thank you. |
| Evie:  | What happens now? |
| Nancy: | You argued well, with much more maturity than you demonstrated when I walked in. And while I respect what you have said, your behaviour cannot go unpunished. But what I have deduced from Ben, Mr Evans and now you, is that this was a crime of passion, so I think a shorter sentence is in order and in the spirit of respect, I will punish you in line with your beliefs. You will be internally excluded for three weeks — you'll report to the learning support room every morning without fail. That seems sufficient enough to also satisfy Ben's parents in light of his injury and will hopefully stay off any complaints which too will make me happy. Then you have a choice. After your exclusion is over, you will either spend every Wednesday lunchtime until the end of term in my debating society or in detention with Mr Evans. I hope you will choose the former as I |

|          | believe it will make *you* happier and allow you to channel your beliefs and opinions safely and learn about the beliefs of others as you said. Thus, the greatest happiness of the greatest number shall be achieved. Is that fair? |
|----------|---|
| Evie:    | Seems a pretty simplified view of communism — |
| Nancy:   | Save it for Wednesdays. And I'd like to see politics on you're A Level form. |
| Evie:    | So, I'm not expelled? |
| Nancy:   | Wouldn't achieve much happiness, would it? And it was never really on the table. But next time – |
| Evie:    | There won't be one. |
| Nancy:   | Can I trust you to put this room back to normal? I'll fetch the learning support officer for a word. |
|          | *Evie nods* |
|          | So, will I see you Wednesday? |
|          | *Evie nods* |
| Evie:    | Thank you, miss. |
| Nancy:   | Okay. |
|          | *Nancy heads out the door. Evie goes to wipe the board. Nancy returns.* |
|          | Oh Evie? Leave the pig. |
|          | *Evie wipes everything but the pig.* |

THE LONG SHOT

(A short film)


Written by

Riya Vivek Thorat













Riya Vivek Thorat is a MA Scriptwriting student at UEA. She was recently shortlisted for the Alpine Fellowship and has worked with Sainsbury Centre for Visual Arts on their Day Release project. She has also been a part of the community chorus for Indigo Giant produced by Komola Collective.
Riyathorat1221@gmail.com

EXT - AD FILM SET - EARLY MORNING

Trucks arriving with light and camera equipment. Tents set up for refreshments. Several people talking at the same time. General hustle and bustle of a busy set in its early stages. People yawning as they patiently wait for their coffees to be ready. The day feels heavy even though it's just begun. PENNY (35,F, average height, brown hair, wearing overalls over a white shirt) arrives in her silver Toyota Corolla. She gets down and immediately rushes over to a truck.

>                    PENNY
>           Stop, you hit the curb, didn't you?

>                    TRUCK DRIVER
>           Sorry ma'am

GIRL (mid-20s, F) walks past, and PENNY turns around to smell her.

>                    PENNY (MURMURS TO HERSELF)
>           Like candied almonds

Someone knocks a baby light over. PENNY rushes over. Picks up the baby light first and then starts yelling at the crew. She gathers everyone up.

>                    PENNY
>           Take a copy of the schedule and the
>           shot list. Let's aim to finish by
>           12.
>                 (in a monosyllabic tone)
>           Let's do this woohoo

The crew all cheer in a monotone to respond back to PENNY. She walks onto set with a writing pad clutched tightly in one hand and her coffee in the other.

CUT TO:


2. INT. - NIGHT - SAME AD FILM SET

Lights set up. The crew stands still. A digital clock shows the time as 1.45am. The walls have been padded with soundproof material. The camera team talking. PENNY (35, F) looks at them weary eyed. She nods and walks away. GIRL (mid-20s, F) approaches her desk.

							PENNY (WITHOUT LOOKING AT HER)
					I know we wrap soon but the camera
					team needs one last shot

							GIRL (SMILING)
					I've got all the time.

							PENNY (ASSUMING SHE'S SOMEONE
							FROM THE CAMERA TEAM)
					Yeah, but most of us want to go
					home. Can you ask them to hurry up?

							PENNY (TYPING ON HER LAPTOP)
					Are you on tomorrow's schedule?

GIRL has walked away. PENNY smells the same scent she did before and looks generally in the direction that the girl went in. She can't really spot her. PENNY gets up and starts stretching. Her bones crack as she looks over to the set. Starts studying it. A bedroom with three walls. All set-up for a scene where a character has to pick up a pillow and then start bashing it up. PENNY is curious and spots the girl again and goes up to her.

							GIRL
					Hasn't this gone on for too long?
					It's almost two.

							PENNY
					It's been a long day, it's fine,
					we have the set until three.

PENNY turns to her.

							PENNY
					So, are you one of the doubles?

							GIRL
					I wish...

The camera team calls out to PENNY. PENNY rushes over. The camera team drone on about how they still need to get the perfect shot. The DIRECTOR (45, M) gets up from his seat and stands next to PENNY.

							DIRECTOR (SHAKING HIS HEAD)
					I can't see it

							PENNY
					See what?

                    DIRECTOR
         My vision. It's not coming to life

GIRL comes and stands behind the DIRECTOR. She starts
imitating his actions. A shrug here, an eyebrow scrunch
and finally the big sigh.

                    PENNY (CHUCKLING)
          Stop!

                    DIRECTOR
          I want to stop, I want everyone to
          go home. Let's pack up.

                    PENNY
          Wait NO what, we can't wrap yet.
          This is the one they specifically
          asked for.

                    DIRECTOR
          It's us vs. them. Who you gonna
          choose?

                    PENNY
          We aren't curing cancer, it's just a
          shot. You've got some good ones
                    (gets interrupted)

                    DIRECTOR
          GOOD ONES? Ughhhh you'll never
          understand true art.

                    PENNY
          High art in a mattress ad?

                    DIRECTOR
          I'm leaving.

The DIRECTOR turns around and exits the set. His Assistant
Directors scramble behind him. PENNY signals one of her
assistants to go follow them.

                    PENNY
          He needs a smoke.
                    (looking at the camera team)
          I need to see the last take

The camera team follows the instruction and then step out for
a short break. The set has gotten empty. Most of the extras
have left. The model also excuses herself.

Through the reflection, we see a hand rest on PENNY'S shoulder. It's GIRL.

                      PENNY
        What do you think? Looks fine to me.

                    GIRL (LOOKING AT HER)
        Yes, looks very pretty

                      PENNY
        Hey, I'm being serious.

                      GIRL
        I guess they could have more
        feathers. The model looks a bit
        tense. Someone needs to go in there
        and give her some directions.

                      PENNY
        So, now I need to be the director.

CUT TO:


3. EXT. - AD FILM SET - NIGHT MOMENTS LATER

Police vans. Ambulances. The crew has gathered around. All of them are being questioned by the police. There is an area that has been demarcated by the police and tape has been put on. A strong hefty MIKE (45, M, POLICE OFFICER) sighs audibly.

                      MIKE
        Is there anyone left inside? How the
        bloody hell did you all take so much
        time?

                      DIRECTOR
        Didn't hear anything. Penny, our
        producer, she's in there.

                      MIKE (YELLING)
        JOHN, get her out, NOW!!!

JOHN (mid-20s, M) stomps onto set. He sees PENNY sitting in the corner. He rushes over to her.

                      JOHN (POINTING AT HIS BATCH)
        Get out, it's an order.

                    PENNY
          Relax, we have the permit, I'm sure
          whoever complained hasn't even
          heard a single noise.

                    JOHN
          They heard everything. And then
          called. Which you should have done.

                    PENNY
          Look,
               (staring at this badge)
          Whoever called is clearly trying to
          mess with us

                    JOHN
          Just come outside

PENNY is lead outside by the CONSTABLE. All of her crew are
standing in two lines. Police officers inspect their clothes
and take notes. PENNY looks in the general direction where
the POLICE OFFICER stands.

                    MIKE
          I don't care how long you've been
          working??? How do you not hear THAT?
               (pointing)

Behind the police tape are evidence markers and blood. A
mysterious body outline.

                    PENNY (STILL TAKING IN HER
                    SURROUNDINGS)
          Ummm... err... the set's soundproof
          so we don't disturb anyone

                    MIKE
          If I hear that word again, I swear
          I'll lock all of you up.

                    PENNY
          I take all responsibility. Don't
          take anyone to the station.

                    MIKE
          Where were you between 12 and now.

                    PENNY
          On-set, with the rest of them
          filming
                    (she drags out the last word)
                    MIKE
          The feathers going everywhere shot?

                    PENNY
          Yes, for the 100th fucking time

PENNY sees someone approaching from behind him.
It's just an outline. GIRL comes up and looks at her.

                    MIKE
          I know all you film people love
          working till the wee hours

                    PENNY
          It's not a choice

                    MIKE
          So you lot heard nothing? Nothing at
          all?

PENNY looks over his shoulder and sees that a crime scene
photographer has borrowed one of their equipment lights to
get a better picture.

                    PENNY
          He needs to return that.

                    MIKE
          I'm blaming it on the caffeine, but
          you all really need to get a grip

                    PENNY
          I can vouch for everyone and say we
          heard nothing.

MIKE leaves. GIRL approaches. PENNY sniffs the air again.

                    PENNY
          Did they question you?

                    GIRL (SMILING)
          They found me.

ACKNOWLEDGEMENTS

The work this anthology presents was written by the 2024 Scriptwriting MA cohort. Our first thanks are to the School of Literature, Drama and Creative Writing at UEA and Egg Box Publishing who brought this anthology into existence. They created a platform giving each student a chance to be published and offer the opportunity for curious students to be involved in the publication process. This has been a privilege.

This year's publication would not have been brought to print without the enduring support and perseverance of Nathan Ashman who guided this process from the start. Working with eighteen writers and eight editors, he has been our linchpin and for that we are so grateful.

Next, we would like to express thanks to tutors and supervisors Steve Waters, Ben Musgrave, Sian Evans and James McDermott, each of whom has tailored this programme to their own unique styles and passed on invaluable knowledge and feedback. A shout out to dissertation supervisors Michael Lengsfield, Christabelle Dilks and Richard Hand too. We thank them all for their respect and wisdom as we have developed our scripts in collaboration with these wonderful writers, many of whom have had their own fantastic works out this year. Without them, we would not be the writers in this anthology.

This year was James's first year teaching at post-graduate level and what a year it has been. From fantastic classes and now dissertation supervision, he has proven what a brilliant teacher he is as well as a writer and person. His play **Jab** premiered in London this year and was a brave and important portrait of lockdown, provoking many conversations and memories about that time. Can you blame us for wanting him to write the introduction?

Then there is Max Fisher, director at Rogue Films, former youth worker and UEA alum. When we met him, his passion and humility is what struck us, not to mention his first-rate film work. From advertisements everyone would recognise to beautiful short films such as **Mouse!**, his talent and precision is admirable. When we asked for suggestions for a foreword writer, he was the first name mentioned and we could not be happier he said yes.

Thanks is due also to our editors John Dakin, Allan Farfan Canales, Ava Hamilton, Rosie Johns, Yavuz Orhun Kiliç, Karen Mayze, Nina Sumerling and Riya Vivek Thorat whose detailed efforts in collating this anthology have enabled its creation.

Lastly, a massive thank you to this cohort, full and part-time, who have offered wonderful work, all-important feedback and friendship. It is a tribute to your hard-work and talent that we have such an impressive and diverse anthology to present. It can be intimidating on courses like these where we must lay before a group the work closest to us, but each of you has made this a pleasure. Now we have reached the conclusion of our course, our names and work are in these pages as testament to our time together.

Here's wishing the very best for everyone's post-post-graduate future!

UEA MA Creative Writing Anthologies: Script Writing

First published by Egg Box Publishing, 2024
Part of the UEA Publishing Project Ltd.

International © retained by individual authors

This book is sold subject to the condition that it shall not, by way of trade or otherwise, be lent, resold, hired out, stored in a retrieval system, or otherwise circulated without the publisher's prior consent in any form of binding or cover other than that in which it is published and without a similar condition including this condition being imposed on the subsequent purchaser.

A CIP record for this book is available from the British Library
Printed and bound in the UK by Imprint Digital

Distributed by BookSource
50 Cambuslang Road
Cambuslang
Glasgow
G32 8NB
+44 (0)141 642 9192
booksource.net

ISBN 978-1-915812-62-9